CW00347483

IAN ALLAN TRANSPORT
LIBRARY

Thornycroft

IAN ALLAN TRANSPORT LIBRARY

Thornycroft

ALAN TOWNSIN

Ian Allan
PUBLISHING

Front cover and Half title page:
The J-type was perhaps Thornycrofts best-known model, remaining in production into the mid 1920s after nearly 5,000 were supplied for military use in 1914-18. In 1921,Thomas Wethered & Sons Ltd proprietors of a brewery in Marlow took delivery of chassis number 9607. It received pneumatic tyres some years later, remaining in service until March 1946 and having earned the name 'Perseverance'. When it was then replaced by a new Sturdy ZE/TR6, it was returned to the Thornycroft works in Basingstoke (see half-title page) and was kept there in good order until 1969, along with other historic vehicles. It later passed to Whitbread, who had taken over Wethered's but returned again to the works for the first Thornycroft Society rally in June 1991, being seen in the cover picture in the works yard it had left 70 years earlier. It is now privately owned. *Thornycroft Society*

Back cover, upper:
The Mighty Antar was best known as a tank transporter or oilfield vehicle, but this Mark III example, chassis number 62821, was supplied to the Royal Air Force in April 1961, it has a Roll-Royce C6TFL six-cylinder turbocharged engine. Its duty was to haul an airfield runway testing trailer capable of imposing a 70-ton load, simulating that of the landing gear of large aircraft. It was transferred to civilian duties in 1963, registered 983 FUL, but in 1998 was purchased by Mike Fincher, being seen here at an AEC Society rally at Gaydon. *Alan Townsin*

Back cover, lower:
Portsmouth Corporation put 10 buses on Thornycroft J chassis into service in 1919. They originally had locally-built bodies (see page 27) but in 1927 nine of these were replaced by similar bodies acquired from the London General Omnibus Co Ltd. No 10 (BK 2986), on chassis number 8457, was retained in this form the body it still carries being by Dodson and dating from 1920 and is nowadays owned by Portsmouth Museums. *Philip Lamb*

First published 2001

ISBN 0 7110 2814 1

© Ian Allan Publishing Ltd 2001

Published by Ian Allan Publishing

an imprint of Ian Allan Publishing Ltd, Hersham, Surrey KT12 4RG.

Printed by Ian Allan Printing Ltd, Hersham, Surrey KT12 4RG.

Code: 0109/A3

Title page:
Thornycroft was already conscious of its history over 70 years ago. No 1 steam van is seen being carried out of the main entrance to the Basingstoke works by a JC six-wheeled lorry to take part in the Lord Mayor's Show held in London on 9 November 1929. The lorry, which had a ZB6 six-cylinder petrol engine, was on chassis 18424 and had been supplied to SPD Ltd the previous June. There was clearly some difficulty with the overhanging tree, which was removed not long afterwards, but the tree-lined frontage of the works made it seem far less forbidding than most industrial premises. *Thornycroft Society*

Below:
This aerial view of the Basingstoke works, thought to date from about 1950, shows it at its full extent, mostly clustered round the original buildings set up in 1898, though a couple of workshops extend beyond the branch railway line. *ATC*

Contents

Acknowledgements

Compilation of a company history is always a voyage of discovery, but never more so than in this case. I spent four stimulating years in the drawing office at Basingstoke as a chassis designer from 1957 until 1961, and even then found it fascinating to witness as well as take part in the workings of what I soon realised was a remarkable firm, even if by then in decline. I was able to build up parts of the earlier story, sometimes from people with direct recollections. It would be impossible to record all the names of those who unwittingly helped in this way, though happily I have been able to resume contact with Don Pearson, a fellow designer, who clarified some queries by looking into his own records. In more recent years, I was in touch with the late Sydney Dack, who provided valuable details of his work in the 1937-47 period.

After being invited to write this book, I raised a number of queries with Chris Tree, Chairman of the Thornycroft Society, and met wonderful generosity in being allowed to borrow many important archive record items, including some donated by members of the Thornycroft family; Mervyn Annetts also helped in this respect. Again many others have built up the Society's collection, among whom perhaps the late Graham Dascombe might be counted as the pioneer student of Thornycroft vehicle history. F. & J. Lawton, of Derby, with a remarkable collection of vehicles

themselves, have similarly pioneered the creation of the Thornycroft Register which lists over 500 reported surviving Thornycroft vehicles, a copy of which also proved helpful. There are also numerous photographs, largely of Thornycroft origin, lent by the Society.

Another important source is the Hampshire County Museum Service, which has taken a strong interest in Thornycroft history, restoring several vehicles itself, as part of its involvement in the Milestones Museum, now open on a site only a short distance from where the works used to stand – Mrs Wendy Bowen was very helpful in allowing me to select photographs. Among individuals, Colin Morris, a fellow writer sharing my fondness for the make, was kind enough to allow me to reproduce photographs from his collection. G. H. F. Atkins supplied some of his own photographs, some recording scenes of 70 years or so ago, while the Ian Allan Library's collection (IAL) originally gave me the idea of such a book. There are some pictures from my own collection (ATC) too.

I have included references to Thornycroft's marine activities in an effort to put the vehicle-building history in context but must acknowledge the value of *100 Years of Specialised Shipbuilding and Engineering* by K. C. Barnaby, which tells the story of the marine side far more fully. It was published by Hutchinson of London in 1964.

Introduction

The Thornycroft story is among the most romantic of all those of the great names in the vehicle business, partly because it spreads so widely. Even before No 1 steam van turned its wheels for the first time in 1895, the family was, by its own skills, becoming woven into the higher levels of society. With both parents as talented sculptors, the 16-year-old John I. Thornycroft set about building a 36ft steam launch in the family studio in Chiswick, then a Thames-side village, in 1859, his father sending him for the best scientific training of the day.

The launch-building business, with emphasis on reaching higher speeds, grew to encompass the construction of the Royal Navy's first torpedo boats and by 1894 the Thornycroft yard had built 300 vessels, including five of the then latest class of fast Navy ships, the destroyer. Then the next generation moved to the road transport sphere, John E. Thornycroft persuading his father to agree to the building of the steam van and then, in 1902, together with his younger brother Tom, finding the possibilities of the petrol engine in both cars and boats of interest. The steam business had outgrown available space at Chiswick, so a new factory was built at Basingstoke from 1898, while the larger ships being built caused a move of shipbuilding to Woolston, Southampton, in 1904.

Motor lorries gradually became a more important line of business than steam wagons or motor cars, and with good relationships with both the Admiralty and the War Office, Thornycroft became a major supplier of ships to the Navy, and lorries, almost all of the famous J-type, to the Army during World War 1, a unique conjuncture. Yet, despite immense prestige, with both John I. and John E. as knights of the realm, the depressions of the 1920s and early 1930s brought harder times. Technological advance helped to mitigate this to some degree, the ability of Thornycroft six-wheeled lorries to travel over poor or non-existent roads helping to build up valuable export business. Yet it was the concept of a high-quality yet simple design of light lorry and bus, the A1 and A2 models, that helped to build up much-needed output volume, with customers of widely varying types, from numerous small businesses to the main-line railway companies.

Larger-sized buses also became quite important for a time, though Tom's sudden resignation in 1934, after some years of poor trading, this latter by no means confined to Thornycroft, removed his enthusiasm for this side of the business. For a time, the range had become very complex, but the firm, perhaps partly because of this excessive diversity, for a time fell a little behind the game in terms of technology. Then, under the management of R. C. Charles, there was a revival of emphasis on simple but well-made models, and success was regained with the Sturdy and Nippy.

The return of war clouds brought work to both Woolston and Basingstoke even before conflict began again in 1939. This time, the vehicle needs were more diverse, and Basingstoke built several types in their thousands. In the course of doing so, much-improved designs of diesel engine were developed. Although simple four-cylinder petrol engines, with their roots going back to the type used in the A1, were still built in large numbers for a further 10 years or so after the war ended in 1945, the postwar emphasis was increasingly on Thornycroft-built diesel engines, standard for most larger models, such as the Trusty range, and now also available in the smaller types. For a time, this latter helped the firm to fend off increasing incursion into the 4-7-ton classes by firms such as Ford and Bedford.

More widely publicised was the development from 1949 of what was then Britain's largest lorry, the Mighty Antar, initially for a specialised oilfield pipeline construction contract but later as a tank transporter. Gradually, during the 1950s, the emphasis swung increasingly to the design and production of specialised vehicles as, bit by bit, the battle was lost for sales of the lighter types of lorry which had provided the firm's bread and butter since the mid-1920s.

The heavy-duty Big Ben six-wheeler was increasingly developed as mainly an oilfield model, the Sandmaster version on massive tyres, to give better flotation under desert conditions, even more imposing than a standard Antar, only to be exceeded in size by the Antar Sandmaster. The Nubian four-wheel-drive TF model introduced in wartime as a military vehicle blossomed into the TFA six-wheel-drive which became a familiar sight at airports all over the world as a crash tender.

Although models for general haulage work continued to be developed, the overall viability of the business steadily declined. Then, just over two months after Sir John E. Thornycroft's death, it was agreed in February 1961 to sell the motor vehicle business to the ACV group, in which AEC was the dominant business. The 1960s were a period of successive mergers and in 1968 Thornycroft became part of the giant but flawed British Leyland Motor Corporation. In 1972 Thornycroft's Basingstoke factory was sold and although the Nubian continued to be built under the Thornycroft name until 1977, the story of its vehicles was virtually over. Happily the name continues into the 21st century as part of the title of Vosper-Thornycroft Ltd, formed in 1966 and still having the Woolston shipyard, a very rare case of continuity since the mid-19th century.

This book seeks to convey, in words and pictures, an outline of the land-based Thornycroft story with some glimpses of the marine story so as to give perspective. The contribution to technology and indeed the life of Basingstoke as a town over three-quarters of a century was immense. For example, Thornycroft provided engineering training for many students who moved on to eminence in other fields in transport or in the Army, this evolving into the town's technical college. It was not an untroubled story but certainly one that deserves its place in history.

Alan Townsin
Steventon, Hants
April 2001

1. Artists and Engineers

When John Isaac Thornycroft was born on 1 February 1843, he could hardly have had a more artistic family background. His parents, Thomas and Mary Thornycroft, were both sculptors, studying art in Rome at the time; John's younger brother William Hamo was also to maintain the tradition. His mother, herself the daughter of an eminent sculptor, John Francis, had exhibited at the Royal Academy when only 21. After the young parents returned to what was then the picturesque Thames-side village of Chiswick, Mary was commissioned by Queen Victoria to produce busts of her children.

Yet Thomas, born in 1815 in Cheshire and at first apprenticed to a surgeon, was also a keen and proficient amateur engineer and metal worker, and it was in his studio in Chiswick and with his encouragement that John began work in 1859 at the age of 16 on a 36ft steam launch, completed in 1862 and called *Nautilus* – it was built in a studio in which Thomas was working on a statue of Boadicea in her chariot, later to play a further part in the story.

By then John had studied engineering at Glasgow University and gained experience in a Clyde shipyard. John I. Thornycroft began the business bearing his name in 1864, and quite a stir was caused in 1871 when boat No 10, *Miranda*, reached a speed of over 16 knots. The Thames was an almost ideal river for the development and sale of steam launches, and though an artist's eye was doubtless of value in producing fine hull lines and elegant appearance, John was more keen to use his scientific training in such aspects as steel construction and efficient propulsion. A succession of launches and other small craft followed, often designed to suit specific needs.

The development of the torpedo brought naval interest in small, fast vessels that could close in to about 600yd of an enemy ship, launch their torpedoes and retire equally quickly. Thornycroft's expertise was directly relevant and vessel No 47, built in 1876, became Royal Navy Torpedo Boat No 1, *Lightning*, the first of many ships' names also later applied to the company's vehicle types. She was 84ft long, displaced about 30 tons and had a speed of 18 1/2 knots. The size of successive designs and the numbers built steadily grew, their construction becoming an important part of what was by then a substantial boat-building business at Church Wharf, Chiswick, though it also built a variety of other craft, such as five steamers for use on the Nile.

In 1886, No 246, a launch, *Boadicea*, a name to recur in the Thornycroft story, was built as an experimental venture.

Below:
Thornycroft's vessel No 47, launched in 1876, was accepted by the Admiralty the following year as the Royal Navy's first torpedo boat, HMS *Lightning*. She was 80 1/2ft long and had a speed of 18 1/2 knots. This view shows her before the torpedo-launching equipment was installed, moored on the Thames, off the firm's boat-building yard at Church Wharf, Chiswick, with a still rural Barnes in the background. *IAL*

Above:
No 1 steam van, completed in 1896, with John I. Thornycroft, the founder of the firm using his name as its title, standing on the left of the picture, and his son John E. Thornycroft, whose concept it was, standing at the wheel, seemingly rather formally dressed for such an occasion. The chain drive to the front wheels is visible, the steering acting on the rear wheels. *IAL*

Below:
This remarkably prophetic articulated lorry, thought to be the world's first, was built in 1898. The steam-driven tractor unit had an under-frame-mounted compound engine, the boiler being behind the driver. At that date, the road vehicle business was called The Steam Carriage & Wagon Co Ltd, based in Hogarth Lane, Chiswick, although Thornycroft was used as a trading name. The youthful figure standing sixth from the right on the semi-trailer was Tom Thornycroft, aged about 16. *IAL*

Torpedo boats for the Navy were being built in much greater numbers by then, a batch of 57 dating from 1885-6 being split between Thornycroft and two other suppliers. The Thornycroft-built boats were of 60-70 tons, with a length of 127ft and their steam engines developed 600-700hp, giving a speed of 21 knots – 18 were still in service in 1914.

Rivalry between European navies was growing and each development led to counter-measures. The result was what at first was called the torpedo boat destroyer – larger, faster and more heavily armed – and again Thornycroft was much involved. In 1893 came No 287, *Daring*, one of the first destroyers, with a speed of 28 knots from its triple-expansion steam engines driving twin screws. This belonged to the A-class, of which Thornycroft built five in the period to 1895, these being about 200ft long and of 220 tons or more, with twin screws and triple-expansion engines of over 3,000hp. In 1895-9, 10 destroyers forming the Navy's D-class were built at Chiswick, the displacement, up to 280 tons, and power to 5,500hp, giving 30 knots. There were also further batches of torpedo boats and one of gunboats, as well as continuing business in launches.

At that stage, steam was still the exclusive motive power for all these craft, although the internal combustion engine was just beginning to become a contender for transport applications. The Thornycroft family could hardly have failed to notice the boats being installed with the new petrol engines to the patented design of Gottlieb Daimler by the Daimler Motor Syndicate Ltd established in London in 1893, using a rented railway arch near Putney Bridge, two miles or so downstream.

Land transport had interested John I. Thornycroft at the beginning of his career, for steam-powered road vehicles had existed since the 1820s but were so severely restricted in Britain as to have almost died out until again permitted to a limited extent for agricultural purposes in 1878, this fostering the development of steam traction and ploughing

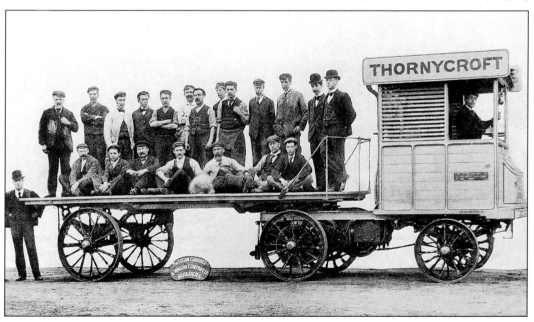

engines. They were subject to the Locomotives on Highways Act limiting speed to 4mph, with a man walking in front. Pressure for its repeal was building up due to growing interest in the early motor cars, making rapid progress in Germany and France, drawing fresh attention to the possibilities.

Thus, in 1895, there was again a young 'Mr John' busy in the Thornycroft household in Chiswick with a new project. This was John Edward Thornycroft, John I.'s elder son, who had been born on 5 September 1872 (so was then aged 23) and also trained as an engineer, it being he who persuaded his father, John I., to agree to the building of a steam-powered van, aided by brothers-in-law Bertie Niblett and Frank Strickland, the latter an engine expert.

The No 1 steam van, as it came to be called, was of 1-ton capacity and was a curious mixture of advanced steam engineering with a 'chassis' only too obviously related to a horse-drawn cart, even if seemingly 'back-to-front'. When it was run under steam in what had been the Thornycroft works yard in Basingstoke a few years ago, the author was surprised by the refinement of the compound vertical steam engine mounted alongside the feet of the driver, who stood on the front platform to drive the vehicle, with the marine-type water-tube boiler behind him.

The engine was quite small and, in fact, similar to those used on the smaller Thornycroft launches of the day, running almost silently at quite high speed, what noise it made masked by the rumble of the iron-shod wheels. It drove the large wheels of the leading axle via reduction gearing to a cross shaft and then by a chain drive, again reducing speed quite markedly, and with chain links not much bigger than used on a bicycle. The steering acted on the centrally pivoted rear wheels, which perhaps seemed natural to a boatbuilder but must have made it tricky to drive in confined spaces, especially as it acted through chains, as on steam traction engines, with considerable inherent free play. Its first long road journey was a 164-mile run from Chiswick to Cardiff

with a load of asbestos, completed in 25 working hours, with no stops for repairs or adjustments. That works out at an average of $6^{1}/_{2}$mph, still illegal at that date, late 1895.

At the time, much of the shed where it was built had been occupied by the plaster cast of Thomas Thornycroft's large statue of Boadicea on her horse-drawn chariot, the front legs of which had had to be temporarily removed to allow room for building the van. The next step was a larger vehicle for which the whole building was needed, but fortunately public interest was aroused by an archaeological find thought to relate to the warrior-queen and a site for the statue was found close by Westminster Bridge – it is still there today. This second vehicle, built in 1897, was a refuse tipper for the local Chiswick council. The road vehicle business was formed into a company, at first called The Steam Carriage & Wagon Co Ltd although using Thornycroft as a trade name, at first based at Homefield Works, Hogarth Lane, Chiswick, near the boat-building yard.

A remarkably prophetic vehicle was built in 1898, this being what would nowadays be called an articulated flat truck, believed to be the world's first goods vehicle to this layout. The tractive unit even had an outline not too far removed from that of a modern vehicle, and the layout was more orthodox with the driven wheels at the rear, under the front end of the semi-trailer, the compound engine under the channel-section steel frame. The boiler was accommodated

in the rear part of the cab, the driver still standing to steer. The load rating was 4 tons and it won a premier award at trials held in Liverpool.

The need for larger premises led to the decision to move vehicle construction to a new factory designed for the purpose. After examining several alternatives, land was purchased adjoining Worting Road, Basingstoke, Hampshire, on which work started on 5 September 1898. The business was to continue at that location until 1972. Steam wagon layout became more stabilised, with the driver seated alongside the water-tube boiler, behind a full-width wrap-round sheet metal dash panel, and the two-cylinder compound engine under the frame, with load capacities from 2 to 4 tons; a 5-ton model added later used a locomotive-type boiler. Municipalities, breweries and railway companies were prominent among customers from the start. Serial numbers reached the 50 mark before the end of 1900, though the wagons were sometimes well out of sequence in order of delivery. By 1904, standard body types were developed, identified by a letter code, SA signifying a

flat lorry platform, SB one with open rail sides, SC with canvas tilt cover, SD with open rail sides and fixed roof, SE lorry with board sides, SF a tipping body, SH a box van and SM a furniture van, this having a lorry platform and removable container that could be conveyed by rail.

The War Office became interested and comparative trials of alternative makes of steam wagon in the Boer War resulted in Lord Kitchener's comment that 'Thornycrofts are the best'. Orders followed, at first on a small scale, but beginning a long spell as vehicle supplier to the Army as well as one of ships to the Royal Navy. Yet, remarkable though it seems with hindsight, a 300-ton torpedo boat, No 322, had been built by Thornycroft for the German Navy in 1898, surviving the 1914-18 war, and steam wagon No 59 was supplied to the German Government War Department in May 1901. Although there was rivalry, at that date there were still quite strong links with Germany – Queen Victoria had died earlier that year and among the mourners was Kaiser Wilhelm, her grandson.

The parent concern was reconstructed as a limited company, John I. Thornycroft & Co Ltd, on 22 May 1901, with John E. Thornycroft as Managing Director and, for a time, the road vehicle business became The Thornycroft Steam Wagon Co Ltd. Experience gained with the Army vehicles in South Africa led to the development of special Colonial models with larger boilers and stronger frames – from 1902 to 1905 about 30 wagons were sold to South Africa, and others to the Congo, West Africa, India, Burma, Singapore and New Zealand, as well as in Europe. In 1902, John I. Thornycroft was knighted, having become a nationally respected figure as a naval architect and engineer. From 1901-7 he was Chairman of the major engineering

firm of William Beardmore & Co Ltd, based in Glasgow, and that concern's subsidiary Stewart & Co, also in that city, built steam wagons to Thornycroft design under licence in the period up to 1911. A manufacturing licence for Germany was also issued to Berliner Maschinenbau AG, to which wagon No 50 had been sold in November 1900. The Belfast & Northern Counties Railway was the first railway company in the British Isles to operate self-propelled buses, taking delivery of two Thornycroft 14-seat steam buses based on standard chassis numbered 82 and 85. One was tested in Belfast in February 1902 before they entered service that spring, running for six years in this form before being rebuilt as lorries, one surviving until 1925. A rather similar vehicle was used by Signor Marconi in connection with his early radio experiments.

A 3-ton chassis was fitted with a converted horsebus double-deck body seating 36 passengers and used experimentally from March 1902 by the London Road Car Co. It had a light canopy to protect upper-deck passengers from cinders from the extended chimney, but the concept proved unpopular and it was withdrawn after about two months. It has also been claimed that a steam wagon sent to Burma even earlier was passenger-carrying; if so, No 63 for Burma Ruby Mines Ltd, dating from August 1901, seems a possible candidate for this honour.

2. Early Petrol Vehicles

By 1902, the petrol engine was well established as a means of propulsion for cars and the smaller sizes of commercial vehicles, proving more convenient than steam even if at that stage less reliable. The repeal of the Locomotives on Highways Act in 1896 was the signal for quite rapid expansion of car use in Britain, even though at first many of the vehicles were German or French. In a brief history of the firm written by John E. Thornycroft, largely responsible for the engine development work carried out at Church Wharf in 1903-8, he refers to De Dion influence and states that the first petrol engines made by the firm, two-cylinder engines of 4in bore and 4³⁄₈in stroke, were made for one of the pioneer British car makers. Thornycroft made its first petrol-engined vehicle, a 4-ton goods model, in 1902, but effort then turned to smaller vehicles.

Tom Thornycroft, younger brother of John E., comes into the picture at this point. He was born on 22 November 1881 – christened Isaac Thomas, he was always known as Tom – and was thus 21 when car manufacture began early in 1903. Although both John E. and Tom were to play major roles in the story, each heavily involved in marine as well as vehicle matters, Tom showed strong early interest in the application of the petrol engine to cars and boats.

The initial range of models offered comprised 10hp two-cylinder and 20hp four-cylinder cars as well as 30cwt and 2-ton lorries, all numbered in the same series as the steam wagons. The engines, of the same 4in bore and 4⅜in stroke as the pioneer units made for sale, were types A2 and A4, with two and four cylinders and swept volume of 1.8 and 3.6 litres respectively. They had atmospheric inlet valves, opening in response to the suction of the descending piston, as then still widely used, being simple though giving limited performance – the normal running speed was 900rpm. On the other hand, the cars were quite advanced in using propeller-shaft drive to the rear axle rather than the chain drive then more usual, though the early goods models used chain drive.

All but one in a run of 20 chassis numbers from 198 to 217 were recorded as 10hp cars, the first two delivered in June/July 1903 though others dated from 1904-7. It seems probable that the run of numbers was reserved for what in later years was called a Stock Works Order, authorising the manufacture of the parts needed, the vehicles of a given type numbered in that range then being built as demand required, sometimes spread over several years, a system retained by Thornycroft to the end of vehicle production. The earliest recorded customer, Mr J. Dent, to whom No 199 was delivered on 29 June 1903, covered about 2,500 miles by September, praising the comfort and quiet running. The 20hp model was also in production from mid-1903 – one of this type and two of the 10hp cars are known to survive.

A very early 20hp petrol engine was modified for marine use in January 1903 and fitted in a very light open launch, *Scolopendra*, which John E. and Tom Thornycroft raced with considerable success in 1903-4, leading to the company's commercial involvement in boat engines – petrol, paraffin or, later, diesel, mainly marinised versions of road vehicle engines.

There were important events relating to the company itself in 1904. The Thornycroft Steam Wagon Co Ltd was absorbed by John I. Thornycroft Ltd and thus the latter concern itself henceforth became the vehicle maker as well as ship and boat builder, a situation that was to continue until 1946.

More significant in practical terms was the transfer of shipbuilding to Woolston, Southampton, where an existing shipyard was taken over. The increasing size of destroyers had made it necessary for them to leave the Chiswick yard without parts of the superstructure so that they could pass under the Thames bridges, completion then having to be carried out downstream. This was uneconomic and the move also made it possible for Thornycroft to build larger ships, soon to become important. The rival firm of Yarrow, then also on the Thames with its yard at Poplar and faced with the same problem, moved to the Clyde. For the first few years, the engine shops at Chiswick were retained, supplying both Woolston and Basingstoke, the latter with petrol engines.

It was decided to set up a boat yard on Platt's Eyot, a small island a few miles upstream at Hampton-on-Thames, initially on a small scale, to meet the continuing demand for launches and other small craft with wooden hulls. Hitherto, such work had been subcontracted, as the Church Wharf yard concentrated on steel hulls. This activity steadily grew and over 1,100 boats were built there over the next half-century or so. Its work tied in with the Marine Motor Department set up in the new London head office, at Caxton House, Westminster. Manufacture of such engines moved to Basingstoke when the Chiswick premises closed in 1908/9.

Left:
The first Thornycroft car, a 10hp, with Tom Thornycroft, then aged about 21, at the wheel – his fondness for dogs continued throughout his life. The sloping bonnet line was characteristic of the early cars. *Thornycroft Society*

Regular production of internal-combustion commercial vehicles got underway in 1904, sales leaflets quoting the C and D types as intended for 2 and 2½-ton loads respectively, though also used as a basis for passenger bodywork. Single-letter alphabetic designations were used quite widely in Thornycroft sales literature of this period, though less common in early internal records, where horsepower ratings or slightly more complex codes were used, based on the gross weight in cwt, with a letter and number, the latter indicating the engine type and number of cylinders. Indeed the factory was apt to use the engine code to signify the car models. The style of radiator at first used and retained on commercial vehicles until about mid-1905 was an untidy-looking stack of horizontal gilled tubes interconnected at the sides, though later the edges were encased.

Among early commercial vehicles was chassis number 370, a 2-ton model with 20hp engine and tank wagon body supplied to the Anglo-American Oil Co in November 1904, while chassis 373 and 374 were for the Cambridge Motor Omnibus Co, the former dating from July 1904 and the latter a 20hp double-deck bus new in May 1905. The variety of motor vehicle output and type of customer increased. To take some examples dating from 1905, chassis 449 was a 20hp landaulette for Sir W. J. Lancaster, while 450 and 451 were 5-ton petrol-engined lorries for J. Birch & Co Ltd.

From about 1905, the runs of chassis numbers allocated to petrol-engined models became longer and more continuous as output expanded, while steam vehicle production began to decline considerably, apart from batches of numbers allocated to D. Stewart & Co, such as 391-409, 425-436 and 687-736, though it is not known how many of these numbers were taken up by output at the latter's Glasgow works.

Below:
Early efforts at petrol-engined vehicles were sometimes far from beautiful – this tanker had a form of radiator consisting of gilled tubing found on early Thornycroft vehicles, cars as well as commercial, though more prominent on the latter. The vehicle is believed to be chassis number 370, a 20hp 2-ton model supplied to the Anglo-American Oil Co Ltd in November 1904. *Thornycroft Society*

Further occasional Thornycroft steam wagons were sold as late as 1911, such as No 781, purchased by Gwynnes Ltd, the pump maker which, incidentally, acquired the Church Wharf premises in Chiswick after Thornycroft left.

A 34-seat double-decker in the livery of the London Motor Omnibus Co Ltd (better known by the Vanguard fleetname later adopted) was exhibited at the Olympia Motor Show early in 1905, this having a new type of four-cylinder engine quoted as developing 'roundly 24bhp', rather less than the 29hp RAC rating implied by its 4¼in bore, the stroke being 5in, giving a capacity of 4.65 litres. This was the B4 engine with mechanically-operated inlet valves, with inlet and exhaust on opposite sides of the engine in the T formation by then usual. Conservative ratings were to remain characteristic of Thornycroft engines of the Edwardian era – the normal running speed of the B4 was still only 900rpm, but a major step forward was the adoption of full-pressure lubrication. There were also B1, B2 and B4 marine versions and much larger C2, C4 and C6 boat engines with 6in x 8in dimensions. The 24hp car, using the B4 engine and with a new and more elegant radiator, became the main type offered by about early 1905, displacing the earlier 20hp. The most prestigious of customers for the 24hp was Princess Christian of Schleswig-Holstein. One of Queen Victoria's daughters, Helena, had married Prince Christian, taking her husband's name on marriage. A picture of the car, with a landaulette body, appears in a Thornycroft catalogue thought to date from early 1906, accompanied by a note reporting that the Prince and Princess had granted a Royal Warrant of Appointment to Thornycroft in appreciation of its 'excellent running qualities', the coat of arms appearing on the front of the catalogue.

Such an honour would take a little time, and it seems likely that the car was an early 24hp, perhaps dating from early 1905. The car bears the British registration number BL 554, a Berkshire mark. No record of this car has been found in the Thornycroft chassis list (perhaps shown under the name of whoever arranged its supply) but No 643, of the later 30hp type, is shown as a limousine with 'H. R. H. Princess Christian' as the customer, the delivery date in that case being November 1906.

Chassis 454 and 455 were 24hp double-deck buses exported to Italy in mid-1905, the first for Signor Benigno Crespi and the second for Societa Romana Tramways – Sr Crespi also took two 20hp single-deck buses. For a time, Italy became a promising market, a licensing agreement being made with Fabbrica Ligure di Automobili di Genoa – one of the preserved Thornycroft cars still carries FLAG on its radiator.

A 20hp 2-ton chassis (465) went to Lisbon Electric Tramways, while the London & South Western Railway took No 480, a 24hp bus with 16-seat body, in August. Nos 481/2 are recorded as a pair of 24hp charabancs for the Midland Railway in July-August 1905, although a photograph shows a Thornycroft with enclosed bus body on a service linking St Pancras with other stations in London that ran for a few months from July 1905; alternative bodies may have been used.

Double-deckers were sold quite widely from late 1905 to 1906, and the 24hp model, by then with the elegant radiator as used on the car version, began to be designated 80B4 – a version with 30hp engine was 80L4 and a combined total of about 60 was built in 1906-7. Nottingham Corporation Tramways began its first bus services with three examples (491/3/7), at least one with Dodson body, in March 1906. The Bristol Tramways & Carriage Co Ltd took the largest single batch of 12 examples (528-39) with which its first motor bus operation began in January 1906. Both these operators experienced some unreliability, Nottingham reverting to horsebuses in 1908 while Bristol, after also trying a batch of FIAT buses, decided to build its own chassis, thus founding the Bristol marque.

At that stage, the whole motor industry and users of its products were on a steep learning curve. Yet Thornycroft vehicles continued to sell quite strongly, and other users

Top:
A Thornycroft's car catalogue dating from about early 1906 includes this picture of a 24hp car supplied to Princess Christian of Schleswig-Holstein, together with an announcement that its excellent running qualities had led to the granting of a Royal Warrant of Appointment by Prince and Princess Christian, which implies that it was built soon after the 24hp was introduced, about early 1905. This refutes the claim that it was shipped to India and dated from 1903 found in some publications, including a Thornycroft volume published in 1946. *Thornycroft Society*

Above:
This bus, seen on a service linking terminal stations in London which operated for a few months from July 1905, bears the name of the Secretary of the Midland Railway. It is thought to be one of two 24hp vehicles built for that concern with chassis numbers 481/2, of which the first was delivered that month. No record of purchase by the MR has been found, so they may have been leased. One was registered in Hampshire as AA 887 and they were returned to Thornycroft.
Hampshire County Museum Service

Above:
The Birmingham & Midland Motor Omnibus Co Ltd was incorporated in November 1904, and in March 1905 this Thornycroft 24hp double-decker was added to the fleet, taking the registration number O 1279, following on from those of nine existing Milnes-Daimlers, though it was actually hired from the London Motor Omnibus Co to which it was returned later in the year. It is seen at Five Ways, operating to Harborne. The style of radiator shown was used on a small proportion of Thornycroft vehicles around that time. BMMO was later to become better known as Midland Red.
Hampshire County Museum Service

Below:
By about 1906-7, car design became quite elegant – note the relaxed driving position. The long bonnet of this open four-seater almost certainly indicates that it was a six-cylinder model, probably a 36hp. Though power output was still very modest by later standards in relation to a capacity of 6.97 litres, there would be ample torque to give quite lively performance with relatively light bodywork.
Hampshire County Museum Service

placed repeat orders. The LSWR took further 16-seat buses, one in 1906 and two in 1907, all on the 24hp or 80B4 chassis, and a final pair in 1908 which were 30hp models. The London Motor Omnibus Co also took 11 similar chassis with double-deck bodies in 1906 but the police, then in charge of bus licensing in London, required drastic alterations, causing the contract to make a loss.

Car sales also continued, with an additional 14hp model known internally as the H4 offered from early 1906 and built up to about 1908, on which a landaulette was built on chassis 540 for Lady Montagu in April 1906. The engine had equal bore and stroke of 3^3/4in, and 2.7-litre capacity; it was unusual at that date in having overhead valves. By November 1906, the three larger car types, all of the T-head engine layout then usual and with 5in stroke, comprised the 24hp model with B4 engine of 4^1/4in bore (4.65-litre), a new 30hp with the L4 unit of 4^1/2in bore (5.2-litre), both the foregoing being four-cylinder, and a 36hp six-cylinder with B6 engine of the same bore size as the 24hp, giving a swept volume of 6.97 litres, introduced early that year. Maximum power had begun to rise but that for the 36hp was still only a modest 45bhp.

An example of the B6 car (677) was sold to Capt Guy Baxendale, with whom Tom Thornycroft entered a car, thought to be chassis number 801 and listed as '4in racing car', in the 1908 Tourist Trophy race. He finished fifth, behind four more powerful cars. A 45hp 7.8-litre six-cylinder model with L6 engine derived from the 30hp L4 was in production from late 1907, one competing to the 1908 Shelsley Walsh hill climb.

Meanwhile, the shipbuilding department produced the first torpedo boat destroyer from the Woolston yard, in 1907 – *Tartar* (ship No 425) of 880 tons, its steam turbines giving a speed of 35.67 knots. It was followed by the generally

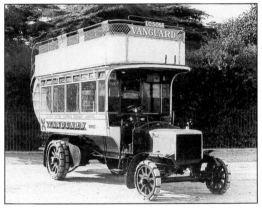

Top:
The Great Western Railway's initials were to appear on a great many Thornycroft vehicles, right up to the formation of British Railways in 1948. However, this 24hp, believed to be chassis number 657 dating from April 1907, was actually delivered to William Rees of the Emlyn Arms Hotel in Newcastle Emlyn, though in GWR livery and operating a route forming part of the extensive network of bus services linked to that company's railway. *Colin Morris*

Above:
The London Motor Omnibus Co, trading as 'Vanguard', took delivery of 11 double-deckers on the 24hp 80B4 chassis during 1906. The firm was soon to have the largest fleet of motor buses in London but decided to build buses to its own design. After it was merged with the London General Omnibus Co in 1908, its former works at Walthamstow, where several of the staff had been trained at Thornycroft, was where the latter's B-type buses were made, later becoming the first works of the AEC concern.
Hampshire County Museum Service

similar *Amazon* and *Nubian* built in 1908 and 1909 respectively, all these being further examples of names to recur as commercial vehicle model names. Nine torpedo boats of around 250-300 tons each were also built in 1906-8, all these forming part of the Royal Navy's expansion that was to prove so vital in the 1914-18 war. Other products of the time included 10 paddle-steamers for the London County Council and *Lady of the Lake* for operation on Coniston Water by the Furness Railway.

Military vehicles had been regarded as important since steam days, even though built in only modest numbers through the Edwardian era. The concept of what amounted to an internal-combustion traction engine, using the large straked rear wheels as a means of maintaining the drive over rough ground, had engaged attention. Four such vehicles, Nos 776-9, were built for the War Office in 1908, their proportions much as the steam version save that the four-cylinder engine, under a large bonnet, replaced the boiler. In deference to continuing War Office unease about petrol, paraffin was used as fuel, then still more widely obtainable in some places than petrol. A Thornycroft paraffin gun tractor won first prize in the 1909 War Office trials, and in 1910 three heavy oil tractors (905-7) were built for the War Office – at that date such a description probably referred to a form of vaporising oil.

By 1908 an advertisement for the Thornycroft range of vans was issued from Caxton House, quoting models of 16 to 40hp and in the 15cwt to 4½-ton weight range. Commercial vehicles were growing in importance. Although some of the larger types of car continued to be sold until about 1911, the car range latterly concentrated on an 18hp (4in x 5in) 4.1-litre four-cylinder model introduced in 1908, type P4, this having side-valve layout – ie all valves on one side of the engine. Users included Lord Montagu, with a landaulette (873), as well as Sir John

Left:
The London & South Western Railway also used Thornycroft buses, though on a smaller scale. These 30hp examples with Hora bodywork, on chassis 770 and 774, supplied for the Exeter-Chagford service, were the last to be delivered, in February 1908, of six 16-seat buses supplied from 1905. The LSWR was incorporated into the Southern Railway formed in 1923, the latter becoming a major user of Thornycroft goods vehicles. *Colin Morris*

Below left:
One of the paraffin-engined tractors of 1908 demonstrating one of its capabilities at the Basingstoke works, hauling the trailer up the sharp slope by means of its winch. The design was based on that of a steam traction engine but with the boiler replaced by a bonnet housing the engine. Just visible in the background is the LSWR branch line to Alton, from which a siding ran into the works. *Thornycroft Society*

I. Thornycroft, whose car (871) of June 1911 had a body in the fashionable torpedo style, but manufacture of cars ceased in 1913, some of the last batches of P4 models (1026-40 and 1042-71) receiving van bodies – a 1912 leaflet quoted the cylinder dimensions of the van version as 4in x 4$\frac{1}{2}$in. Average car output had run at under one per week, of all types, over the decade of production; competition within what was still a very limited market was intense and Thornycroft's products were not sufficiently outstanding to break out of the small niche of users into larger-scale output.

The commercial vehicle business was far better suited to the flexible production methods possible in a relatively small business, a situation which was to allow Thornycroft

to survive in difficult times on several occasions over the years. A range of 16hp two-cylinder chain-drive models largely built as vans, catalogued as types R and S, of 15cwt to 25cwt weight rating, and A and B, of 2 and 2$\frac{1}{2}$ tons, was offered from about 1908 to 1914. The 16hp two-cylinder engine was the M2 of 4$\frac{1}{2}$in bore and 6in stroke, giving a swept volume of 3.13 litres. They had the radiator set almost directly over the front axle, as also applied to the 30hp four-cylinder commercial vehicle chassis of that time, types C and D, again of 2 and 2$\frac{1}{2}$ tons and with the same basic chain-drive chassis, though the wheelbase was increased to suit the longer engine.

In chassis number records, the models were designated on the basis of load rating in cwt and engine type, giving type designations such as 20M2 (which was rare), 30M2 and more frequently 40M2 and 50M2, or 40L4 and 50L4 for the four-cylinder 30hp types. They were produced in batches with the above types intermingled, and their growing success is indicated by the way in which these tended to become larger.

The first of this range shown in the records was chassis number 780, a 40M2 box van for Kennedy Motor Co delivered in June 1908. Ten, and then a further 10, followed, with 30 early in 1909, 20 and another 30 by 1910 and then 50 (these with chassis numbers 948-997) in the autumn of

Below:
Car production continued until 1913, output latterly being concentrated on the 18hp 4.1-litre four-cylinder P4 model shown in two-seat form in this view. The radiator shape gave a foretaste of the styles used on commercial vehicles of the late 1920s. *Hampshire County Museum Service*

Above:
A market in which Thornycroft found a firm demand was in the production of medium to light commercial vehicles, which retained chain drive until 1913. Many of them used a 3.1-litre two-cylinder engine, the M2, which established a good reputation – it was housed under an appropriately short bonnet. This example for Leeds Industrial Co-operative Society, dating from May 1910, is thought to be chassis number 900, a 2-ton 40M2. *IAL*

Below:
The four-cylinder commercial vehicles of the period from around 1910 to 1913 or so mostly used the 5.2-litre L4 engine, though the chain-drive chassis was generally similar to that used for the two-cylinder models, with radiator positioned over the front axle but with a longer bonnet. This one retained Edwardian elegance though it was certainly not aerodynamic. *Thornycroft Society*

that year, these batches interspersed mainly with P4 cars. Then there was a run of 27, with one chassis renumbered from an earlier batch, and then what seems to have been meant as a run of 100 beginning at chassis 1076, but the last of that run (1175) was built for export as a 40L6, with the big 7.8-litre six-cylinder engine, possibly as a fire engine, followed by a 50M2 as number 1176.

In 1913-14 there were two runs of 125 each, followed by what was probably meant to be 50 beginning at chassis 1856 but interrupted by the war and ending at chassis 1902, a 50M2 delivered in January 1915. There were thus about 575 of this range of models, the most important group produced in the period up to 1914.

Users included numerous trade and retail concerns, local and national, including such household names as Oxo and Cadbury's. The London & North Western Railway took several deliveries of 50M2 lorries.

The 40L4 and 50L4 were favoured for charabancs by operators such as Caernarvon Motors Ltd, Lake District Road Traffic Co and the Llandudno Coaching & Carriage Co. The War Office took two 40L4 lorries (901/2) in May 1910 and developments along these lines were soon to become more important.

Exports were of growing importance, notably for Australia, largely 40M2 or 50M2. A special Colonial Model M using the L4 engine was introduced, this having the front axle on a pivoted transversely sprung mounting, an early venture in design to suit operation over uneven ground. Some of a batch of 30 built in 1913-14 went to countries such as India or Nigeria, but others still in stock in August 1914 were taken by the War Office.

3. War Brings Expansion

As is often the case, war, or the threat of it, sharpened the demand for advances in technology and was to bring major expansion to several manufacturers of motor vehicles, Thornycroft prominent among them. The War Office, foreseeing a large-scale need for Army transport, issued a specification in 1911 for a 3-ton motor lorry with the emphasis on sturdy construction, reliability and the ability to deal with gradients and poor roads. In practice, the specification was such that vehicles built to meet it were rated to carry substantially more under normal civilian use.

Although makers were free to use their own types of engines and other major components, subject to overall War Office approval, the specification, founded on experience in trials over difficult terrain, was based on what became regarded as 'good practice', calling for a shaft-driven live rear axle rather than chain drive, for example. Overall, the specifications had quite a strong influence on the design of British commercial vehicles for at least the next 15 years. A Government subsidy scheme was announced to encourage the purchase of such vehicles by civilian users with the aim of building a reserve of approved vehicles which could be drawn upon for military use when needed. A premium payment of £50 was made to assist purchase, with an annual subsidy of £20 for three years subject to satisfactory maintenance.

Thornycroft, with its close liaison with the War Office, was among the first makers to introduce suitable models. A new model H with a gross load rating of 4 tons was announced in February 1912, using the '30hp' L4 engine but higher-built and with sturdier chassis than the C and D. It was quoted as having a live axle though the type of axle gearing was not given. This may have been because it was a matter of dispute with the War Office, which favoured a bevel drive, which implied a double-reduction type at the

ratio needed whereas Thornycroft preferred a worm drive as cheaper to produce.

In the event, an initial batch of 24 chassis of H, J and K-types of basically similar design, numbered 1177-1200, was built and mostly delivered between August 1912 and May 1913. No 1177 was a K, having a double-reduction axle, sold to Pickfords Ltd; reputedly, this was the chassis that performed very successfully in the 1913 War Office trials, leading to approval of the type. Succeeding numbers were a mixture composed largely of H and K-types, with customers such as Westminster Borough Council, which took two H-types as tipping and watering wagons, though 1182, 1189 and 1194 were K-types supplied direct to the War Office. There were four J-types, which had the worm-driven axle, in this series: 1191 and 1195-7. The first was exported and the others went to S. G. Martin & Co, J. W. Rudd and Barrow-in-Furness Corporation.

A further 100 subsidy chassis (1355-1454) began deliveries in the spring of 1913, this time 50 J and then 50 K, though chassis 1435 of the latter was in the event completed as a J. Most of the J models went to commercial users, including some bodied as charabancs for the Llandudno Coaching & Carriage and Isle of Thanet Electric Supply fleets, while about half the K-types were built for the War Office. A few from both batches had not been delivered

Below:
The batch of 50 J-type chassis of 1913-14 included eight recorded as having charabanc bodywork. This photograph, reproduced in a Thornycroft circular of 1914, shows one with a Leeds registration, U 2351. By elimination, it seems likely to have been either chassis 1356 or 1393, both delivered in the spring of 1914. The wheels were of the conventional spoked type of the time, standard at that date. *Thornycroft Society*

in August 1914 and these too were delivered to the War Office, as explained later.

Military output thereafter settled on the J-type, soon to become Thornycroft's best-known model, remaining so until the mid-1920s. It gained and retained a reputation for outstanding durability, many examples remaining in use far longer than could have been foreseen when they were built.

A list of the commercial vehicle types then available for general sale issued by Thornycroft in the early months of 1914 continued to include the 16hp two-cylinder A and B models with M2 engine and the 30hp four-cylinder L4-engined model C and D, together with 'Narrow B' and 'Narrow D' versions, plus the Colonial 30hp Model M. All of the foregoing retained chain drive.

In addition, there was a new range of models of which deliveries began in the latter part of 1913, with shaft drive to

Above:
Late in 1913, a new range of models covering the range between 1-ton and 2½-ton capacity appeared, having a new 3½-litre four-cylinder engine, the T4, and propeller-shaft drive. Three of the 2-ton AT model, chassis numbers 1631, 1638 and 1640, were supplied in January-February 1914 to East India Tramways Co Ltd for operation in Karachi, and are seen here soon after entering service. The operator reported favourably on the fully enclosed engine and drive, excluding dust.
Thornycroft Society

a live rear axle, the RT of 1-ton load capacity; ST (1½ ton); AT (2 ton) and BT (2½ ton). All these had a four-cylinder 20/24hp engine, type T4, of 3½in bore and 5½in stoke, giving a swept volume of 3.47 litres – it had overhead inlet valves directly above the side exhaust valves, a form of engine to be favoured in several Thornycroft models of the early 1920s. These '-T' models were intended as successors to the previous R, S, A and B chain-drive models respectively, although the A and B continued to be available briefly. The new range had a general appearance similar to the J-type, somewhat scaled down. Following a prototype RT box van and another T4-engined chassis, numbered 1328/9, it seems that a production batch of 250 was planned, beginning at chassis number 1580, an ST lorry for Hull Corporation being delivered in October 1913, but in August 1914 the war intervened and there were intermittent gaps after 1773, the highest-numbered chassis delivered at this

Left:
The 1914-18 war brought a need for expansion of Thornycroft's Basingstoke works, which was one of the top five British suppliers of military lorries. This scene is thought to date from 1915, and in addition to the rows of J-type lorries lined up in the works yard there is evidence of building work as additional workshops are constructed.
Hampshire County Museum Service

Above:
The J-type was perhaps the most famous of all Thornycroft's
models, providing reliable transport for the Army in 1914-18
and much favoured for civilian transport in its aftermath.
This scene shows a group mostly having mobile workshop
bodywork, posed with their drivers.
Hampshire County Museum Service

stage being 1802. There was a similar range of customers to
that for the previous comparable types, with the LNWR and
GWR among railway users and Carter Paterson, the express
parcel delivery specialist, taking a large fleet.

During 1913 a new engine described as the 40hp was
introduced for the J-type, retaining the same $4^1/2$in bore as
the 30hp L4 engine as used in the early subsidy H, J and K,
but with stroke increased from 5in to 6in, and thus of 6.256-
litre capacity. This was the M4 engine, a four-cylinder
version of the much-respected M2 two-cylinder unit used in
the smaller goods models as built from 1908. Its T-head
layout, with inlet and exhaust side valves on opposite sides
of the cylinders, was by then beginning to fall out of general
favour. However, it was well suited to what proved to be its
main task in the wartime J-type lorry, with the emphasis on
low-speed pulling power and with all items needing regular
attention readily accessible.

The J-type chassis as sold for civilian use in 1914 was
quoted at $3^3/4$ to $4^1/2$ tons gross load rating. The M4 engine
was also used for a new model, the Q-type, of generally
similar design to the J but rated at 5-6 tons when put into
more general production postwar. A batch of 20 chassis was
authorised in 1914 (numbered 1830-49), about half being
completed in the winter of 1914-15, the rest not going out
until 1919-21.

When what later became known as World War 1 began on
4 August 1914, most of the subsidy models that had been
sold to civilian users were impressed for military use during
the following weeks, and, in addition, stock vehicles and
chassis of other types, including those awaiting delivery,
were handed over directly to the War Office. Output was
immediately turned to production for the Government, an
initial batch of J-type chassis being put in hand, even before
the official War Office order came through. The Basingstoke
factory was by then under the management of Bertie Niblett,

a key figure since the days of the original No 1 steam van.
However, he volunteered for military service, in due course
rising to the rank of Colonel, remaining in the Army in
postwar days, influential in guiding its vehicle policy and
thus still playing a significant role in the Thornycroft story,
as will emerge in a later chapter. John E. Thornycroft took
direct charge of the Basingstoke factory in addition to
Woolston and Hampton, overseeing a time of major
expansion to meet wartime needs as well as direct
involvement in many projects. He was knighted in
recognition of his achievements.

After the variety of output since motor vehicle production
began, there was now almost complete standardisation,
J-type models emerging in an almost unbroken flow, most of
them with standard Army lorry bodywork, though some
carried anti-aircraft guns or specialised bodywork. There
were minor changes in design during the production run,
most notably the replacement of the cast spoked wheels
usual on most commercial vehicles of that era by the disc
wheels, having a conical shape with eight large holes, which
became characteristic of the model. Extension of the
Basingstoke works was put in hand, new workshops being
added several times during the wartime period, extending
the premises to 21 acres. Women workers were recruited and
amounted to 35% of the 1,550 employed there.

The first batch of J-types built in wartime was of 100
chassis numbered 1906-2005, delivered to the War Office

Above:
Some J-types were fitted with anti-aircraft guns, ground jacks being provided to brace the vehicle against the recoil. This scene posed in later years shows the example preserved at the Imperial War Museum, on chassis 3817, dating from July 1916. The distinctive pierced disc wheels, standard on military J-types and most postwar examples, were quite unlike those of any other maker's products. *Thornycroft Society*

Below:
Among the most colourful wartime exploits in which Thornycroft was involved was the 1915 expedition in which two 40ft motor launches built at Hampton were shipped to Africa, to be hauled overland to Lake Tanganyika. They
were carried on trailers built at Basingstoke by traction engines, accompanied by the J-type stores lorry seen in this view of those involved. The trip took five months, including 150 miles of great difficulty through the bush. They then successfully attacked the German gunboats in possession of the Lake. It seems almost certain that some of the plot of the story and film *The African*

from September 1914 to the end of the year. Almost unbroken military production through the rest of the war began at chassis number 2218, the first of a run of 200, in February 1915. Then a massive series of 1,900, roughly equal to Thornycroft's entire prewar vehicle production, numbered 2419-4318, was turned out between April 1915 and February 1917 – in the event, a small minority of these were released to civilian users whose needs were considered essential. Another 1,200 (numbers 4419-5618) followed before the end of that same year, and then a further big run began at number 5719 in January 1918.

The end of the war in November 1918 broke the hitherto virtually continuous sequence of vehicles delivered for military use. The last number shown as supplied to the War Office was 6971, delivered a month after the war ended, but the cut-off of deliveries left a gradually increasing proportion free for sale to civilian users from about a hundred numbers before that, these soon finding buyers. The continuous run of J-types, thereafter all sold to civilian customers and delivered in 1919-20, continued to chassis number 7968, this sequence of chassis numbers thus adding up to some 2,250 vehicles, of which about half were supplied to the War Office, and it seems likely that many of the remainder might at first have been so intended.

After the war, Thornycroft quoted the wartime output of J-types as 5,000 but this was slightly 'rounded up', the exact figure depending on whether factory output or the numbers actually delivered to the military are counted, including those diverted or impressed from civilian customers. Even so, if those probably intended for the Army but sold to others in the period just after the war are counted, the total would run well over that figure. Thornycroft was thus firmly in the 'big league' of British commercial vehicle makers.

Rare breaks in the wartime J-type numbers occurred as a result of the India Office favouring the X-type, a model

similar to the J in its general design, including the M4
engine, but designed to carry a slightly lighter load – in
postwar form it was quoted as a 3½-ton model as opposed
to the J-type's 4¾-ton rating. First came a single X-type
lorry, chassis 2418, supplied to the India Office in
December 1915. Then there were 100 more, 4319-4418,
delivered between 1916 and 1918 and thus running well
behind J-type deliveries. The numbers 5619-5718 were
reserved for 100 more X-types for India but these were not
built until just after the war, the first few accepted for India
or the colonies but the rest, completed in 1919, being sold
off, some to dealers.

At Woolston in the 1914-18 period, the 3,850 employees
built some 29 destroyers, together with three submarines and
11 other vessels. Four of the destroyers, built in 1918, 1,300-
ton ships of 37,000hp, were to serve through World War 2,
not being scrapped until 1945-8 – one was appropriately
named *Woolston*. There were 114 coastal motor boats, 202
tenders and patrol boats built to the company's designs,
some by licensees.

Considerable co-operation existed between the factories,
the Basingstoke works and other concerns making 3,010
depth-charge throwers, a Thornycroft invention, fitted to
most Royal Navy ships involved in anti-submarine duties, as
well as general munitions.

The coastal motor boats revived the concept of a small,
fast torpedo boat, the hull being scaled up from a racing
boat, *Miranda IV* of 1910, one of a succession in which Tom
Thornycroft had competed very successfully. This work,
personally supervised by John E. Thornycroft with the

Above:
The India Office chose the X-type, lighter than the J but using
larger-diameter front wheels and having the same 6½-litre M4
engine, for 100 vehicles built in 1916-18; a further batch was
on order when the war ended. Some were supplied complete
with trailers as seen here. The 2-ton load rating was very
conservative – after the war, the X-type was sold as a 3½-ton
model. *Thornycroft Society*

Top right:
The end of the war brought military orders to an abrupt halt,
but civilian demand for vehicles was at first very strong. When
Portsmouth Corporation placed its first six motor buses in
service in August 1919, it must have seemed entirely fitting
that the order from this city, with its strong naval traditions,
went to Thornycroft for J-type chassis, on which Wadham
Bros of nearby Waterlooville built 34-seat double-deck bodies
– they are seen lined up in that town. *Colin Morris*

Right:
The J-type soon became familiar in civilian form in the early
postwar years – this example for Hanson Bros Ltd had a cab
of typical style as produced for general sale. The problem was
that, although the model was widely respected, potential
users could obtain ex-military examples at far less cost than
new ones and which were often in sound condition, such
reconditioning as needed still not bringing the cost anywhere
near that of new vehicles. *Colin Morris*

Above:
The postwar BT 2½-ton model, as built from 1920, was basically as had been introduced in 1913 though the engine was now the AB4 of 4.53 litres. This example with dropside body, on chassis number 8366, dated from October 1921.
Thornycroft Society

benefit of Tom's direct experience, was based on research into hull design aimed at skimming across the water, on which his father had taken out patents as early as 1877. The final form of engine for the CMBs was the Thornycroft Y12, a 12-cylinder vee-form petrol engine of some 36-litre capacity, developing 375bhp at 1,600rpm.

With the return of peace, the prospects for commercial vehicle sales seemed quite promising, for the demand for road transport both in Britain and abroad had increased greatly, the war having shown what was possible. Such prewar vehicles as survived were often in poor condition but the capabilities of models such as the Thornycroft J to give reliable service even in difficult conditions had been amply demonstrated. The firm's good reputation extended to most parts of the British Empire, then at about its peak in extent, and indeed to other areas such as the Middle East, China and South America where British influence was strong – Thornycroft had opened branches or set up agencies dealing with both marine and vehicle business in almost all countries with sales potential.

Demand at first seemed encouraging and further substantial batches of existing types were built, notably runs of 750 J-types in 1919 to mid-1922 and 500 in 1922-6, the latter including derivatives of that model. Similarly there were another 100 X and then 300 with numbers reserved for a second but the latter had run only to 176 when output of this type ceased in 1925. Brewery companies were again prominent among users, an association that was often to continue with later models. The Great North of Scotland Railway, which had been allowed to buy three new J-types in 1916, followed these up with six more in 1919, all bodied

as 18-seat buses by the operator. The Great Eastern Railway received six new J-types with 28-seat bodies in September/October 1919.

Perhaps the most apparently promising customer choosing J-type chassis for passenger applications in this period was the British Automobile Traction Co Ltd, set up as a bus-operating offshoot of the big British Electric Traction Co Ltd combine, which had opened a branch serving the Thames Valley area in 1915. In its early days, BAT tended to support manufacturers on a geographic basis to some degree, and Thornycroft was selected as supplier to this branch, 23 new chassis being supplied, probably from stock, in 1919-20 and fitted with a variety of bodies in BAT's workshops in Reading, only 17 miles from Basingstoke.

To cater for the demand for models in the 2½-ton class, the BT was reintroduced in 1919, its general design much as offered in 1914 but now with a new engine, the AB4, with cylinder bore increased to 4in while retaining the 5½in stroke, thus increasing the swept volume to 4.53 litres. It retained the overhead inlet and side exhaust layout of the T4 but had been developed to improve efficiency. A run of 200 starting with chassis number 8169 began delivery at the beginning of 1920, followed at chassis 8669 by another of 300, completed save for the odd vehicle by mid-1923. In 1921 the model gained the RAC's Dewar Trophy after competing in a 1,260-mile trial. It proved popular for local delivery work, the London & North Western Railway again being among users.

After the initial postwar surge in activity, sales began to drop and by 1922-3 British industry was cutting back as the economic climate worsened. More crucially for Thornycroft and the other big wartime lorry makers, the availability of ex-military examples severely undermined the demand for new models of almost identical types. Vehicles such as the J-type became available in large numbers, some having been little used and in good condition. However, such was the rugged nature of the model that even those recovered in outwardly poor state could be reconditioned relatively cheaply. A Government organisation for the disposal of ex-Army vehicles was set up at Slough and dealers were able to offer reconditioned ex-military J-types for about a quarter of the price of new ones.

The ironic consequence was that quite large numbers of J-types entered service with goods and passenger fleets in the early 1920s without bringing more than marginal work or income to the Thornycroft factory. When British Automobile Traction decided to convert its operations in the Thames Valley area into a separate company, the Thames Valley Traction Co Ltd, in July 1920, it continued to standardise on Thornycroft vehicles for additions to its fleet until 1926. By that date 103 examples on J-type or closely related chassis were in service, yet the only examples bought directly from Thornycroft were the 23 purchased by BAT in 1919-20, although it seems probable that in some cases new parts were obtained to allow many of the vehicles to be rebuilt to later specification. The balance were mostly on ex-Army chassis, although some came from other operators' fleets. Some vehicles for various operators were reconditioned and fitted with new cabs and bodywork at Basingstoke.

4. Finding Success amid Adversity

Thornycroft's position in the early 1920s was one of great prestige and, initially, financial strength resulting from its expansion to meet the wartime demands for both ships and lorries in 1914-18. Yet this apparent security was to be severely tested when the period of inflated demand collapsed, as shown by a succession of annual losses. The firm was by no means alone in facing difficulties. In particular, Leyland Motors Ltd was not finding survival easy and for a time around this period discussions were held on the possibilities of a takeover of that firm by Thornycroft. Had this gone through, the implications for later history might have been immense.

The shipyard at Woolston turned to a variety of civilian vessels – cargo ships, ferries, tugs, pilot steamers and even cattle barges. At Hampton, there was a return to the roots of the business, with pleasure craft of renewed importance, whether sea-going 100-ton motor yachts or small motor cruisers for use mainly on the Thames. Another range of related products was engines for marine use, a well-known and very successful example being the modest Handybilly two-cylinder petrol or paraffin unit of $7^1/2$-9hp, often used as an auxiliary for sailing craft, which went into production in 1918 and continued to be made until 1947.

Sir John E. Thornycroft wrote a far-seeing paper on the future design of road vehicles for the Institute of Transport

in May 1922. It acknowledged the fuel economy of diesel engines, for example, but correctly judged that they were unlikely to be found on lorries 'at an early date' – he spoke with some authority, having built a 150bhp diesel engine, admittedly for a stationary application, during his days at Chiswick in 1903-8. He foresaw the possibilities of containers but considered the type then favoured by the railways was too heavily built. He also advocated mechanical means of loading or unloading, another development not to become common until much later in the century – by 1925, a power take-off was offered for the heavier models.

Another development he mentioned was the trolleybus and, following use of what were probably ex-military J-type chassis by Shanghai Tramways, to which undertaking 14 English Electric motors were supplied direct in 1921, Thornycroft built new chassis for three other projects in 1922-4. Chassis 9671, a J, was delivered to Railless Ltd in

Below:
A J-type lorry with power-driven crane, a commonplace idea today but an advanced one nearly 80 years ago. It was posed in Worting Road, Basingstoke, not far from the works and at a location often chosen for official photographs, for a paper on future design trends given in May 1922 by Sir John E. Thornycroft, who was particularly interested in the role for mechanical handling equipment. *ATC*

Left:
Shanghai Tramways developed its own design of trolleybus, based on extensively modified Thornycroft J-type chassis, as seen in this 1922 illustration. The chassis are thought to have been ex-military – 14 sets of English Electric motors and controllers had been supplied direct to Shanghai in 1921. The layout, with driving position ahead of the front axle, became widely adopted 30 years or so later. *ATC*

Bottom left:
The forward-control W-type with 6-ton load capacity was introduced in 1922, but was built only in small numbers, the layout not proving popular at that stage. This example, supplied to Dawson Manufacturing Co of Oldham in August 1923, on chassis 10028, had the second production BB4 engine, the overhead-inlet side-exhaust unit of just under 7 litres that succeeded the M4 so familiar in the wartime J-type. *Thornycroft Society*

Below:
The lightest model in the range in the early 1920s continued to be the BT, introduced in 1914 but having the AB4 engine from 1919. This passenger example on chassis 8895 was supplied to Birkenhead Corporation in February 1923 and had a Strachan & Brown 20-seat body, equipped to permit one-man operation. Numbered 17 (CM 4686), it was to prove the only Thornycroft bus in that undertaking's fleet. *Colin Morris*

Top right:
The Patrician was closely related to the BT, but modified to suit growing demands for passenger models to have a more car-like character. These two, chassis 10283 and 10284, were supplied via Thornycroft's Shanghai branch to Shanghai & Hong Kong Hotels in July 1924. The limousine effect was somewhat illusory – the sides were open, with pull-down weather protection. *ATC*

Right:
The BX in standard form was outwardly similar to the BT it replaced, the main difference being the adoption of a four-speed gearbox. This example, on chassis 10993, was delivered to Hovis Ltd in October 1924, the livery and lettering seeming very 'modern' in relation to the traditional looks of the vehicle. *Thornycroft Society*

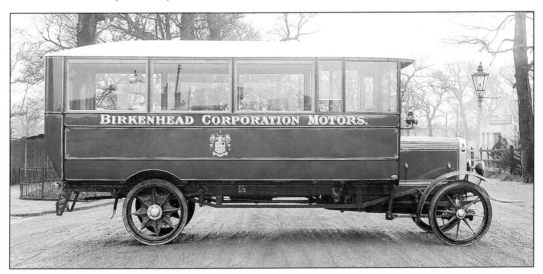

June 1922 and was probably the basis of a vehicle that firm supplied to Ramsbottom UDC the following month. An X chassis, 9839, became what was claimed to be the first trolleybus on pneumatic tyres, in Georgetown, Malaya in 1924, and two BT chassis, 11434/5, were also built as a basis for trolleybuses that year. The idea then lay dormant until 1930, when another approach was tried, as explained later.

However, recovery from the very difficult early 1920s was based on a combination of more orthodox developments. The Q-type chassis, which had briefly begun production in 1914, came into the picture a little more strongly as a heavier-duty equivalent to the J, rated at 5 tons, from 1920 with an initial postwar run of 100, numbered from 8069. There was also one initial example of the W, chassis 8153, built in late 1922, this being a forward-control version of basically the same model, though rated at 6 tons. At that stage, both still had the M4 engine.

Sales of the BT continued with another run of 300 (beginning at 10069) from mid-1923 to late 1924, although that figure included about 10 examples of a separate but closely related type. This was the Patrician passenger model, sharing the 4.53-litre AB4 engine and other mechanical

features of the BT, seating up to 20 passengers on a 14ft wheelbase and at first offered as a charabanc. The use of a name for identification itself was a new development, the first example, 10124, being listed as 'BT charabanc (Patrician)' but thereafter simply as 'Patrician' with no type letters. The aim was to produce a more car-like vehicle, with slightly lower frame line, pneumatic tyres as standard and more flowing bonnet line. By then, pneumatics, hitherto confined to cars or small commercial vehicles, had been fitted to a few BT and X models with passenger bodies and quite soon became usual for passenger vehicles of similar weight, though goods applications took longer to develop.

The AB4 engine, by then developing 41bhp at 1,500rpm, was linked to a four-speed instead of three-speed gearbox, with other revisions, for its use in the new BX type, of 2^{1}/$_{2}$-ton load rating with 13ft wheelbase introduced in mid-1924 and superseding the BT.

A new passenger model, the Boadicea, also using the AB4 engine and four-speed gearbox, of similar form and appearance to the Patrician but longer, with 16ft wheelbase and seating up to 32, was included in BX production batches. The first of these, of 100, began at 10919 and included 33 Boadicea, though the proportion was less in later runs of 100 BX-series chassis, of which there were four until a final 50 were built in 1926.

Some operators favoured the BX itself for bus work. The Stalybridge, Hyde, Mossley & Dukinfield Joint Board took delivery of eight BX buses with 26-seat Vickers bodywork early in 1925 – they began an unbroken run of choice of Thornycroft buses for that municipal undertaking, based in

Above:
The Q-type was introduced in 1914 as a slightly heavier-duty version of the J, suitable for 5-ton loads and initially with the T-head M4 engine, but by the time this 1925 example, chassis 11400, was built, the BB4 engine had been adopted. The radiator was slightly deeper than on the J-type. *Colin Morris*

Below:
A forward-control bus version of the J, called the JB, was introduced in 1924, intended to cater for the demand for a model suitable for operation in London. Although this photograph taken for Brush, which built the body on the vehicle shown, dates from May that year, the chassis was a J-type, originally placed in service by British Automobile Traction in 1920, shortly before its services in the Reading area were transferred to the newly formed Thames Valley concern, but rebuilt to forward-control, possibly using some JB parts, before receiving the body shown. It seems that the signwriter had made an error, the registration number actually being DP 2606. *Colin Morris*

the northeast corner of Cheshire, which was to last until 1936, by which date 104 had been purchased, including seven with an acquired business.

Another run of 500 chassis numbers was allocated for the J-type, beginning at 10369 in late 1922, but it took until the spring of 1926 before it was completed, having grown to cover several variations. The heavier Q and closely related W were built in more cautious runs, one of 50 starting at 10019 at about the same time being completed in a little over a year and then followed by another from 10869.

From about late 1923, a new BB4 engine, again with overhead-inlet side-exhaust layout, gradually became standard for the heavier models, generally being described as of 50hp rating though the $4^3/_4$in bore gave an RAC rating of 36.1hp. The stroke remained at the 6in dimension of the M4 which it superseded, the swept volume becoming 6.97 litres, putting this among the larger four-cylinder engines then on offer in road vehicles.

Above:
Dublin United Tramways Co (1896) Ltd began its bus operations with this JB model in 1925, initially bearing fleet number 1. It had Hall Lewis 30-seat bodywork and pneumatic tyres, an option then quite new on a bus of this size. As with the Boadicea, Thornycroft was unusual at that stage in fitting the front wheels with the concave face on the outside – although there were no front brakes to accommodate, it can hardly have helped the steering geometry. *ATC*

By that date, the radiator style adopted for the heavier models was not as tall as that of the J in its wartime form, having radiused corners for the grille opening, though the separate top and bottom tanks were not disguised in its outline.

The BB4 engine was adopted for the J, now listed as a 4-ton model, and the Q, now offered in 5 or 6-ton versions – the W designation faded out, though the 6-ton model continued to be available with forward control, still quite a rare choice on Thornycroft vehicles. By 1925 the bonneted Q was being offered as a 12ft-wheelbase tractive unit for use with semi-trailers made by Carrimore Six-Wheelers Ltd, the combination rated at 10½ tons, one being used to deliver Higson's Ales. Publicity for it reminded potential users of Thornycroft's pioneer articulated steam vehicle of 1898, and doubtless reflected Sir John's continued faith in the concept, but the industry was still not yet ready for large-scale acceptance of the idea.

Also powered by the BB4 engine from late 1923 was the JB forward-control half-cab bus chassis built as a variant of the J with numbers in the contemporary main series for that type, beginning at about 10425. This was available as a single-decker, with 16ft 6in wheelbase for bodywork of up to 27ft 6in length and seating up to 38, or in 15ft 6in-wheelbase form for double-deck bodywork. The latter, with 50-seat open-top body, was approved by the Metropolitan Police for operation in London. This would have implied meeting tight standards in relation to gearbox noise in particular, yet the specification leaflet quotes only the standard four-speed sliding-mesh gearbox.

A number of JB models with Dodson bodywork to this specification were sold to independent operators running London services, most notably Cambrian which had a fleet of 13, these and other Thornycroft double-deckers in such fleets later passing to the London General Omnibus Co. When it was agreed in 1926 that the Thames Valley concern would operate services in the Uxbridge area on behalf of LGOC, 20 of these vehicles were acquired by Thames Valley. In addition, a number of the latter's own J-types were rebuilt in 1924-5 to JB specification and fitted with new Brush open-top bodies, in that case of 54-seat capacity.

JB single-deckers were built for several fleets. Although no model name was applied to the JB chassis, drawings of what were described as standard types of omnibus on this chassis appeared in the descriptive leaflet in a manner common at the time – in practice, construction was subcontracted and most major operators favoured their own choices. Those for the JB were named 'County', 'Jason' and 'Juggernaut', this last a strangely unattractive choice.

When the Dublin United Tramways Co began bus operation in 1925, a Thornycroft JB with Hall Lewis 30-seat body was allocated the first number – it had pneumatic tyres, an option by then available for the single-deck version. As with the Boadicea model when so fitted, they were unusual

in having disc front wheels of a concave shape instead of the convex form almost universal on commercial vehicles of British design when on pneumatics. Five more with bodies built in the DUT workshops soon followed. Other JB models were exported, notably to Australia – by then Thornycroft had overseas branches in Argentina, Australia, Brazil, Canada, China, Denmark, Egypt, India and Malaya, as well as agencies in many other countries.

A long-wheelbase version of the bonneted J, specifically intended as a passenger model, was also offered, an October 1925 leaflet designating it as the 'J Long' in a manner to be characteristic of several Thornycroft types over the following years. It had a 16ft 6in wheelbase, as compared to the 13ft 7$\frac{1}{2}$in at that stage standard for what was called the freight version, and was derived from the JB forward-control model, having a similar form of frame, stiffened by bracing members on the underside. Northampton Corporation's first five buses of August 1923 had been J-types with this form of frame, and Aberdeen Corporation, which had standardised on Thornycroft buses from 1920, mainly J, though with five BT charabancs in 1923, was a user of the J Long, taking four on pneumatic tyres in 1925.

However, the numbers of the various models described being sold in the early to mid-1920s, well respected though they

Left:
The third and seventh production A1 chassis, 11023 and 11027, were the first to be completed as buses, and were delivered to Northampton Corporation in October-November 1924. The bodywork was built by a local concern, York, Ward & Rowlatt Ltd, seating 16 passengers, a recognition that the 20-seat capacity claimed for the initial 11ft 6in-wheelbase model was barely realistic. *ATC*

Below left:
The solution to the space problem in the A1 when used as a bus came in November 1925 with the introduction of the A1 Long model with 14ft wheelbase. This example on chassis 12376 was delivered the following month to the Devon Motor Transport Co. Ltd, set up by Cdr F. T. Hare and building up a substantial fleet of Thornycroft buses but which was sold to the National Omnibus & Transport Co in 1927. *Colin Morris*

were, were barely enough to save the Thornycroft commercial vehicle business from danger of collapse. It was the revival of the subsidy scheme by what was now sometimes called the War Department that triggered a fresh line of success, although the overall merit of the model that resulted greatly broadened its appeal. This time, attention was concentrated on a 30cwt capacity and the specification called for a more nimble type of vehicle.

Thornycroft's response was the A1 model, introduced in September 1924 with a first batch of 10 (11021-30) following chassis 11020 of the same type, kept at the works as the 'station lorry'. It was of very simple design yet high quality. The newly designed four-cylinder engine was the FB4 of 3¼in bore, 5in stroke and 3.62-litre capacity. This time it had side valves but, like Thornycroft's larger engines, full-pressure lubrication. An output of 36bhp at 1,500rpm was quoted with 'up to 40bhp at increased revs'. Thornycroft publicity also quoted the ability to reach 40mph, at which speed the engine would have been running at 2,400rpm. This was quite fast by contemporary standards for a commercial vehicle, though about 30mph was probably more 'natural' – officially, all traffic was then limited to 20mph. It was quite a sweet-running as well as an economical engine.

There was a single-plate clutch, smoother in action than the cone type used on the larger types, and the four-speed gearbox had a less cumbersome action. The rear axle had worm drive. Externally, the model had a well-proportioned look, with the radiator having a smoother outline than previous models. The writer was told by a Thornycroft employee of that era that a man and boy could assemble an A1 in a day with minimal mechanical aids – there was only one pipe on the chassis, from the dash-mounted petrol tank to the Solex carburettor.

The model looked what it was: simple and relatively easy to drive – perhaps the most obvious weak spots in the original specification as judged with hindsight were the brakes, originally acting only on the rear wheels, and the nominal continued standardisation on solid tyres, though with pneumatics as an option from the start. In practice, few seem to have been sold on solid tyres, even the Army now favouring pneumatics because of better performance over soft ground, and they became standard from 1925, while four-wheel brakes were also adopted from 1926.

The A1 chassis cost £480 in basic form but a subsidy totalling £120 was payable over three years to the purchaser if the vehicle was maintained in good order for possible purchase in the event of a national emergency. This helped to bring Thornycroft into a much bigger market, and the model was soon attracting orders from a wide variety of users from the railways and petrol companies to numerous small businesses. Production batches of 200, 300 or 400 then followed in rapid succession and by the end of 1925, the total of A-series models in use reached 1,000.

A passenger version of the A1 was also built, at first retaining the same 11ft 6in wheelbase but with slightly longer frame and quoted as a 20-seater, though this implied a very tight internal layout. The first were a pair for Northampton Corporation delivered in October 1924. More significant was a delivery of 40 to the Great Western Railway in April-June 1925 on chassis numbers 11461-11500, these having 19-seat bodies by Vickers. The GWR built up the largest fleet of directly owned buses among the British main-line railway companies in the period up to 1929, of which 90 were Thornycroft, including 62 of the A1 type, in addition to its large fleet of goods versions. Another important A1 bus user was Devon Motor Transport Ltd, and fleets were exported to Bombay, Calcutta and South African Railways. The need for a longer version of the same basic design, notably for passenger work, led to the introduction of the A1 Long announced in November 1925, this having a 14ft wheelbase.

The A2 and A2 Long were added to the range in October 1926, these being 2-ton versions using the same basic design as the A1 models, but with uprated springs and tyres. The longer versions of the chassis allowed a more spacious seating layout in passenger versions, although even the A2 Long was still listed as a 20-seater, with gross body and passenger load limited to 2½ tons – the unladen weight of complete examples was usually under 3 tons. The extra length also allowed bodybuilders to avoid the rather stubby look inevitable with the short A1. The A1 and A2 remained in production with minor changes until 1931, the combined production exceeding 5,000, and were still a familiar sight until after the 1939-45 war.

A quite different military specification of that period was for a four-wheel-drive gun tractor, based on a prototype built in Royal Army Service Corps workshops in 1923 from German components captured at the end of the war. Thornycroft produced a vehicle meeting the requirements, given the model name Hathi, meaning Elephant. It used a GB6 six-cylinder petrol engine of 4¾in bore and 6½in stroke and 11.3-litre capacity and dry sump lubrication. It had the same overhead-inlet side-exhaust layout as the AB and BB engines and had been developed by the marine department for use on motor yachts etc. It was to be the first of a succession of six-cylinder engines using these cylinder dimensions, even though of widely varying nature, that were to be used on Thornycroft vehicles over a span of about 40 years. The transmission comprised a three-speed main gearbox and two-speed auxiliary, from which shafts led to the front and rear worm-drive axles. To transmit the drive to the front wheels a set of bevel gears was incorporated in each swivel

Above:
The Hathi gun tractor, with four-wheel-drive and an 11.3-litre six-cylinder petrol engine, was a remarkable *tour de force*. This scene shows what was probably one of the first pair built in 1924 being tested under the eyes of Army officers by hauling a field gun and its limber over muddy ground before completion of the bodywork and painting. Note the chains fitted to all wheels. *Thornycroft Society*

Below:
Involvement in advancing technology was just as strong on water. Warship building had almost ceased after the 1914-18 war years, but Thornycroft was given an order for one of two destroyers to act as prototypes for future construction, with a largely free hand in its design. The result was HMS *Amazon*, launched at Woolston in 1926, a 1,350-ton ship reaching 38 knots on its sea trials in 1927, as shown here. There were four 4.7in guns and six torpedo tubes. She served in the Home fleet and Western Approaches, then being used for training before being scrapped in 1948. *IAL*

unit. It was claimed to be able to negotiate 3ft gulleys, and a winch could exert a pull of 5 tons.

A total of 35 Hathi models were built, the initial pair (11431/2) going to the War Office in November 1924. Production ran intermittently from July 1925 to March 1927, there being further batches of 12 and then six for the War Office, three for the Admiralty, eight for Australia, three for South African Railways and one for the Sudan Government.

There was a gap in destroyer construction after those in hand in 1918 were completed. However, in 1924-5 the Admiralty requested Thornycroft and Yarrow, as the leading destroyer specialists, each to build a prototype embodying the lessons learned during the war, giving each a free hand within the overall specification. Thornycroft's answer, launched in 1926, was *Amazon*, of 1,350 tons and with turbines of 39,500hp, giving a recorded speed of 37.96 knots.

5. Fresh Ideas and Growing Variety

The success of the simple side-valve layout used in the FB4 engine of the A1 led to the development of larger engines of similar form – the good low-speed torque was a characteristic well suited to heavier types of vehicle operating at the low speeds then permitted. Another A1 feature standardised for subsequent Thornycrofts was the direct attachment of the gearbox.

Two such engines, both again with four cylinders, appeared in 1926. The first, the HB4, had 4³/₈in bore and 5¹/₂in stroke, giving swept volume of 5.42 litres. Output was quoted as 46bhp at 1,500rpm, rising to 50bhp. Later in the year came the MB4, this being a direct replacement of the BB4 overhead-inlet side-exhaust engine used in heavier models since 1923 and retaining its 4³/₄in bore, 6in stroke and 6.97-litre capacity. Its output was 58bhp at 1,500rpm, rising to 60bhp at higher speeds. All these were still very modest figures.

Below:
The KB 3-ton bonneted goods model, first seen in 1926 and having the new HB4 engine of 5.4-litre capacity, retained a traditional appearance though the solid-tyred wheels were of a new design. This was the prototype, 12926, with brewer's dray body, sold to H. & G. Simonds of Reading in June 1926. Thornycroft Society

The HB4 engine was the common factor in new mid-range models in the 3-4-ton class. Two prototypes chassis were built, having HB4 engines numbers 1 and 2. The first, 12926, was a KB 3-ton goods model on solid tyres and with other features generally similar to existing types in the range, with foot brake still acting on the transmission, only the handbrake acting on those at the rear wheels. Chassis 12927 was a passenger model, type LB, but this was almost wholly new, with a completely different chassis to the goods equivalent. It was completed in March 1926, and extensive test runs were made before a Vickers bus body was fitted in June, the vehicle being retained until late 1927. Work on it had been begun the previous year by a design team led by Tom Thornycroft, by then resident director at Basingstoke.

The most obvious new feature of the LB was the lower build, with frame top face 2ft from ground level, the chassis being cranked over the front and rear axles; the rear axle had an underslung worm drive. The 16ft 6in wheelbase allowed room for a 28-30-seat body with the bonneted layout of the standard model. This also had the foot-controlled transmission brake and handbrake on the rear wheels, although front wheel brakes were an optional extra.

General sales of both KB, starting at 13353, and LB, at 13453, began in late 1926. The 100 KB mostly found buyers

by mid-1927, a dozen going to the Anglo-American Oil fleet, with a further 200 beginning at 14741 completed by late 1929 – many went to oil companies, breweries and various export markets.

The LB story was brief, with barely 30 built and sold, ending in 1928, yet its chassis laid the foundations for some of Thornycroft's most popular passenger models, as will emerge later. A further model, the UB, appeared before the end of the year, having the new and larger MB4 engine – this required the radiator to be mounted slightly further forward, almost flush with the dumb-irons. Chassis 13456 in the above LB series was completed as the first UB, a demonstrator with Northern Counties 26-seat body, registered OT 4329. Perth Corporation was the first customer for UB buses, 13476 and 13482 being supplied in May 1927.

A November 1926 price list quoted the passenger range as the A1, A2 and LB series only, the previous models having been dropped. In practice, the LB too was already fading from the scene, the larger-engined UB proving much more popular – at least one LB was re-engined. A new variant was the UB Forward, with driver alongside the engine, a run of 25 beginning at 14463 early in 1927 – the Perth and Kilmarnock municipal fleets both took batches. A bonneted UB series began at 14490, this finding favour with the SHMD Joint Board and Wigan Corporation, the latter already having four LB buses. In all, SHMD took delivery of 18 UB with Northern Counties 26-seat bodies in 1928, followed by eight UBX forward-control 32-seat versions in 1929.

Early in 1927, a slightly lower-built version of the A2 Long model became standard, though here the changes were not enough to warrant a change of designation. This variant was soon being built in runs of 100 at a time, most becoming small buses or coaches, often for independent concerns all over the country as well as for export, though others became vans for various types of user.

Forward control was coming into wider favour, and the PB goods model of this layout was virtually an equivalent to the KB bonneted model, though rated at 4 tons. A batch of 50 PB models (13603-52) for the Great Western Railway

was in hand by November 1926, and was soon followed by more, its design suiting that company's needs for operation in urban areas, the layout producing longer body space, while retaining the manœuvrability given by the short 13ft wheelbase.

A major national event was the General Strike of 4-12 May 1926. Many individuals involved in road transport in one way or another saw the possibilities of providing alternatives to the railways and other strike-bound large organisations. Among them were Tom Thornycroft, then in overall charge of the company's Basingstoke premises as Works Director, and his wife, Gladys.

They decided to put some buses on the road, initially working from a garage in Reading Road, Basingstoke. A company, Venture Ltd, was registered on 17 May, quite separate from the Thornycroft business and with Mrs Gladys Thornycroft as Chairman, though sadly she died in 1927 at the young age of 33, Tom becoming Chairman. The first two buses were A1 20-seaters registered new that month, but others were bought from Thornycroft's stock. A network of local routes was built up and a garage built nearer the town centre, in Victoria Street. For the first two years or so the buses owned by Venture were A1 or A2 models before the choice turned to larger single-deckers, but it was convenient to try out vehicles with new features on Venture services from time to time as well as for former demonstrators to be sold to Venture. For several years there was a degree of fluidity between the rolling stock of the two organisations.

Meanwhile Sir John E. Thornycroft, Tom's brother, continued his interest in new developments mainly related to goods vehicles, the rigid six-wheeler now attracting his attention. This interest was shared with his former colleague Colonel Niblett, by then in charge of vehicle development at the War Office. The original impetus for the rigid six-

Below:
The 4-ton PB goods model, with HB4 engine, was nominally of forward-control layout but the version as built for the first batch of 50 for the Great Western Railway in the winter of 1926-7 had a bonnet-like cowl of almost conical form. *IAL*

Above:
The LB passenger chassis, also having the HB4 engine and introduced in 1926, permitted lower build than had been possible on earlier models, giving an elegant appearance as well as easier entry. This example for the Isle of Thanet fleet, registered KO 2780 and on chassis 13479, was one of a pair dating from June 1927 and had bodywork by Hall Lewis.
Colin Morris

Below:
The UB model had another new engine type, the MB4 of just under 7-litre capacity, which required the radiator to be moved forward as compared to the LB, establishing the
front-end proportions to be followed by subsequent bus types. This was the first, on chassis 13456, having MB4 engine number 2; it was registered OT 4329. It had Northern Counties 26-seat bodywork to a style with uneven pillar spacing also found on a United-bodied Thornycroft LB demonstrator, so may have been to a Thornycroft specification. It was sold to Harrison & Richardson, of Hamsterley, County Durham, trading as the Venture Bus Co, predecessor of Venture Transport (Newcastle) Ltd.
Thornycroft Society

Left:
Venture Ltd was registered to operate bus services in the Basingstoke area in the aftermath of the General Strike of May 1926. This enterprise was based on the initiative of Tom Thornycroft, Works Director of the Thornycroft concern, but the two businesses were quite separate. This scene at the garage built in Victoria Street, Basingstoke, shows two of the A2 Long buses with 20-seat bodywork by Wadham Bros typical of the early fleet. No 5 (OT 4785) with chassis 14127 on the right dated from March 1927 and No 9 (OT 8485), 14690, on the left, from May 1928. *Thornycroft Society*

Below left:
Thornycroft took up the concept of the rigid six-wheeler with enthusiasm, co-operating with the War Office in developing its cross-country capabilities. The A3 model introduced in 1926 was developed from the A1, retaining its 3.6-litre FB4 engine, but incorporated the rear bogie as well as an auxiliary gearbox. An early example is seen climbing a 1 in 2½ gradient on Bagshot Heath, using chains on the bogie wheels to improve the grip on the soft surface. *IAL*

Below:
The layout of the patented Thornycroft rear bogie as developed for the A3 and related models is seen here. Pairs of springs were mounted one above the other on each side and centrally pivoted to the frame. Each of the rear axles was pivoted to the ends of the pairs of springs so as not to twist them even when traversing very rough and uneven ground, this giving exceptional ability to keep all wheels in contact with the surface. *ATC*

wheeler had come from the United States and was related to early use of pneumatic tyres for buses, but the War Office was more interested in its potential for travel over soft or rough ground.

Thornycroft developed a patented form of rear bogie, using two pairs of leaf springs, those on each side pivoted centrally one above the other and with the ends of the springs attached above and below the axles by pivoted links in such a way that the difference in level of adjacent wheels on each side of the vehicle could be about 2ft. A key feature in its success as a cross-country vehicle was that the springs were not caused to twist and thus the driven wheels maintained contact with the ground even on very rough terrain. The brakes acted on the bogie axles, with none on the front axle, as was common practice in the early days of six-wheelers.

Fitting such a bogie to a modified A1 chassis, retaining the FB4 3.62-litre four-cylinder engine and four-speed gearbox but with a two-speed auxiliary gearbox attached to its rear face and using large-diameter wheels, produced a model initially described as the A1/RSW at its introduction in 1926. The first example, 12925, was supplied to South African Railways in February 1926. Later that year, the six-wheel version became a separate model, the A3.

The A3 had a wheelbase to the centre of the rear bogie of 12ft and was quoted as being capable of carrying 3 tons on good roads, reduced on rough ground. It proved capable of climbing a 1 in 2½ test hill with a rough though firm surface on an Army test ground at Aldershot, using chains on the bogie wheels, albeit very slowly. Clearly such a vehicle had strong appeal not only as an Army lorry but also for the many parts of the world where roads were poor or non-existent, such as in parts of India, where it was chosen by the Army, or Australia – in those days the British Empire was still very extensive and British influence often strong elsewhere. Just under 500 were built in the period up to 1930, a creditable figure when the British Army intake of vehicles was low, even though its involvement in tthe model's development remained strong.

Experience in operation of six-wheelers showed that there was a demand for a heavier type of vehicle and also a need for more power, especially when covering terrain such as soft mud or loose sand. The XB model, of which the first chassis (14538) was completed in January 1927, again for South African Railways, was a heavier-duty design, intended to carry up to 5 tons, with pneumatic tyres as standard. It used the then new MB4 engine of just under 7 litres, again with main and auxiliary gearbox, the combined assembly being bolted directly to the engine. The overhead worm rear bogie was a heavier-duty version of that on the A3. Batches of 10 and 25 followed in 1927 and then three of 50 each by the end of 1929, with SAR as the biggest user – it soon proved to be in steady demand. The standard model had a 14ft 3in mean wheelbase but the XB Long with 18ft wheelbase was added in November 1927 – a bonneted layout was used, as was to remain usual on models mainly intended for export. The XB was aimed mainly at countries like South Africa, though a few were sold in Britain.

Up to 1927, the heavier-duty end of the home market for

Above:
The XB, of which the first was built in January 1927,
catered for the demand for a larger type of six-wheeler than
the A3, suitable for commercial transport in countries with
poor or non-existent roads, and having the then newly
introduced 7-litre MB4 engine – the chassis being tested over
a muddy track was of the 18ft-wheelbase XB Long type.
Thornycroft Society

Thornycroft goods vehicles still largely depended on very
traditional two-axle bonneted models on solid tyres. The
J-type, of which examples were still being built that year,
ended with a total output of 7,149 since 1913; the Q, latterly
with MB4 engine, was built up to 1928. The JJ, of which a
demonstrator was running in July 1927, was clearly intended
as a successor to the J, using the new side-valve MB4 engine,
though rated at 5 tons, and thus extending into the range of the
Q model – solid tyres remained standard although pneumatics
were now available. A new CC Forward 7-ton model also
using that engine was added in May 1928, but only 14 were
built. The goods range as advertised that month consisted of
the A1 (30cwt), A2 (2 ton), KB (3 ton), PB Forward (4 ton), JJ
(5 ton or 6 ton), CC Forward (7 ton), plus the A3 (3 ton) and
XB (5 ton) six-wheelers.

Six-cylinder Buses

For a time in the late 1920s, Thornycroft's vehicle-
manufacturing business was in quite a healthy state, the A1
and A2 attracting orders from large and small users, while
the development of six-wheel models and chassis intended
specifically for bus duty were helping to extend what were
already wide-ranging markets at home and abroad.
Shipbuilding activity was generally rather quiet, although an

order for six destroyers for Chile, all launched during 1928,
was won against stiff competition. Sir John I. Thornycroft,
the founder of the business, died on 28 June 1928.

The passenger range became quite complex for a time,
though some models proved short-lived. A further new four-
cylinder passenger model was the SB, using the 16ft 6in-
wheelbase low-frame chassis and HB4 engine, basically as
introduced for the LB, added to the range in January 1927. It
was quoted as a 24/26-seat coach model, the first of the type,
chassis 14460, being sold to Dengate of Rye in May.
Thirteen more were sold up to the spring of 1928.

Far more publicity was being concentrated on new models
with six-cylinder engines. The first to appear was the A6,
given the model name Lightning, announced as a 20-seater
although it had a 15ft wheelbase and was later quoted as a
20/26-seater. The side-valve engine, type YB6, was of $3^3/_4$ in
bore and $5^1/_4$ in stroke, giving a swept volume of 5.7 litres.
Power output was quoted as 70bhp, the specification
including a seven-bearing crankshaft and timing gears
placed at the rear. There was a unit-mounted four-speed
gearbox and four-wheel servo brakes. An initial batch of five
A6 models (14968-72) was built in late 1927. Chassis
number 14969, registered OT 5948, with Wadham Bros
coach body, was running by August 1927, retained by the
company until 1932 when sold to Venture Ltd.

The quite racy tone of the Lightning sales leaflet made a
remarkable contrast to the sober style usual for Thornycroft
publications, quoting 'effortless acceleration', 50/60mph
speed, 'hour after hour at 45mph with the utmost comfort
and freedom from vibration', and climbing the 1 in $4^1/_2$
gradient of Lynmouth Hill at 11mph – one can imagine
someone, perhaps even Tom Thornycroft himself, enjoying
the confirmation of this last item.

The model was built initially in production runs of 75 at a time from early 1928, but sales success did not match that of the A2 Long; as a 20-seater, a chassis price of £725 was expensive. Independent operators purchased the type in ones and twos and some were exported but very few went to larger concerns. The Great Western Railway took three with Buckingham 15-seat folding-roof coach bodies in May-June 1928, used on extended tours and then a special service linking Oxford and Cheltenham. The type was in production until 1932, a total of 266 being sold.

The A6 may have taken its designation from its six-cylinder engine, but the first batch of the A4, which was derived from the A3 cross-country six-wheeler, initially retaining its standard 12ft mean wheelbase but having the 5.7-litre YB6 six-cylinder engine, began deliveries just afterwards, in October 1927, with 26 numbered from 16120, South African Railways being the main recipient. It had been found that extra power was helpful when negotiating soft

ground although the refinement of the six-cylinder engine may also have been a factor in its design, as it was intended for both passenger and goods use – as a bus it was quoted as a 14/20-seater and was built in modest numbers over the next few years. Forward-control versions were included in the range. An A4 lorry was used for an expedition across the Kalahari Desert in June-July 1929, proving reliable and more economical on fuel than a lower-powered vehicle used on a previous expedition. By 1928, a 15ft wheelbase and 26-seat capacity were being quoted for the A4, making the model more directly comparable to the A6 two-axle model.

Possibly the best-known of all of Thornycroft's bus types was the BC Forward, introduced at the November 1927 Commercial Vehicle Show held at Olympia. In essence, it amounted to a UB Forward chassis into which another new six-cylinder engine was fitted. This was the ZB6 of 6.9-litre capacity, with $4^{1}/_{8}$in bore and $5^{1}/_{4}$in stroke, the side-valve layout and general design being similar to that of the smaller-bore YB6 unit. Power output was at first quoted as 85bhp but this was dropped to 82bhp in 1929 publicity material. Unit construction of the four-speed gearbox and the provision of four-wheel brakes with vacuum servo were up-to-date features, though the latter initially still used a transmission brake linked to the front brakes, and the rear wheel brakes were operated only by the handbrake. There was also a 'plain' BC model of bonneted layout, but the emphasis had swung to forward control for bus work.

Below:
This Lightning A6 coach was displayed at the 1927 Olympia Show and had a hint of contemporary American car design about its looks, not entirely out of character in relation to its 5.7-litre six-cylinder side-valve YB6 engine. It was on chassis 14971, one of the initial batch of five of the type and was used as a demonstrator before sale to Lewis Horne in March 1929. Coach body design was then in a transitional stage, the folding canvas top remaining but with glass side windows and centre gangway. *Thornycroft Society*

The Show vehicle was chassis 16068, fitted with ZB6 engine number 1. It had a Hall Lewis 32-seat body. Also at that show were new six-cylinder models from ADC, the short-lived joint enterprise of AEC and Daimler, and, more especially, Leyland, which introduced its all-new Tiger single-deck and Titan double-deck models at the same November 1927 Show, providing strong competition.

The initial production batch for the BC Forward was of 50 chassis, starting at 16273. The Isle of Man Railway took delivery of 18 in May-June 1928, one of which is the only BC known to survive today – there were also four A2 buses. In addition, the prototype BC Forward, 16068, was purchased in April 1929. Most had the fleetname 'Isle of Man Road Services' and a company of that name was set up in 1930 following an amalgamation with other bus operators on the island, bringing a further 18 A2 buses to the combined fleet. The Isle of Thanet Electric Supply Co, which operated trams and buses in that part of Kent and was already a firm Thornycroft customer, received the four lowest-numbered production BC Forward buses, also in May-June 1928, two of which were notable in having open-topped double-deck 48-seat bodywork by Hall Lewis, although the model was not being marketed as a double-decker at this time. The LNER, with a growing bus fleet, took two at that stage, as did Perth Corporation, while South African Railways received six.

The BC Forward in original form, like the UB Forward, had an unusually high driving position, set back slightly so that the gear lever could act directly on the gearbox, a feature inherited from earlier models but creating problems when allied with bodywork having the low floor level by then in favour and requiring a rearward-facing front seat behind the bulkhead. An increase in crankshaft dimensions after a year or so may also have been significant, and a tidier front end with gear change of the remote type as used by

most other makers was also adopted – from about 1929 more new customers were obtained.

The normal-control BC was allocated what might have been meant to be 50 numbers from 17031, but only the first 31 from this batch, plus 17066 (for Brazil), appear as sold in the records, the first going to Camplejohn Bros in May 1928 but only about six others being sold that year, most dating from 1929. Many were exported, notably two for Bloemfontein Municipality in South Africa, one for New Zealand and five for Overseas Motor Transport Co, but, rather nearer home, Pitlochry Motor Co had two and H. C. Chambers, of Bures, one.

A significant development was the introduction of heavier-duty six-wheel passenger models than the A4. By then two other British makers were well established as builders of six-wheeled buses, Karrier having a single-decker at the November 1925 Show and Guy with a double-decker in mid-1926, both supplying several municipal fleets in 1926-7. Thornycroft's first design for such a model, the EC, was quoted in the November 1927 price list, a sketch of a bonneted six-wheel single-decker appearing on the cover; an EC Forward was also listed. Small production EC batches were built, all with ZB6 engines, one of 10 (17081-90) delivered in May 1928 and another of 19 later that year and into 1929, the first and most of the second being for South African Railways.

Meanwhile, a forward-control prototype six-wheel bus chassis, number 16350, designated FC Forward, was running

Below:
The bulk of sales in the 20-seat class stayed with the A2 Long; this bus with Challands Ross, body for use on a group of services run by the London & North Eastern Railway in the Durham area, was first licensed in October 1928. No 127 was on chassis 15404 and was registered XV 5129. The LNER bus livery was green with an imitation grained wood finish to the waist panels. *G. H. F. Atkins collection*

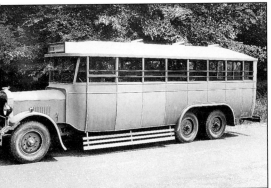

Above:
By 1929, the closed saloon look had become more usual –
this Lightning A6 with Duple body may have been intended for
display at the Commercial Motor Show that autumn. *ATC*

Left:
The A4 combined the A6 front end, complete with the YB6
engine, with the rear bogie of the A3. This 28-seat bus was
exported to the Thornycroft branch in Brazil in July 1928.
Thornycroft Society

Below:
The first production example of the BC Forward, perhaps
Thornycroft's best-known bus model, was 16203, fitted with
Hall Lewis 32-seat bus body, one of four for the Isle of Thanet
fleet delivered in June-July 1928. *Thornycroft Society*

Top:
This photograph of a BC Forward model with Challands Ross bus body is dated August 1928 and conveys the characteristic appearance of Thornycroft forward-control passenger models of that period. Note the unusually high steering wheel, with column protruding through the front dash panel. The unladen weight was 5 tons 5cwt. *ATC*

Above:
The LNER followed an initial pair of BC Forward buses with a batch of 12 with Hall Lewis 32-seat bodies dating from November 1928. No 130 (XV 1191), on chassis 17726, is seen posed for photography in Worting Road, directly outside the Thornycroft works, the clock tower just visible through the trees. Although the 6.9-litre ZB6 engine was housed in quite a short bonnet, the gear lever linkage protruded through the dash on early examples of this model, requiring the front pair of passenger seats to face rearwards. *IAL*

by June 1928, with front-end similar to the BC Forward but with a rear bogie, again with the Thornycroft form of suspension but in this case with underslung worm drive. The chassis was just under 29ft long, with 18ft wheelbase, allowing for 40-seat bodywork. The prototype was bodied by Strachan & Brown and, after use as a demonstrator, was added to the Venture fleet by 1930.

A production batch of 50 forward-control six-wheel bus chassis was sanctioned, numbered 17421-70, and in the event this included 11 of a double-deck version, designated HC. Liverpool Corporation had put about 70 six-wheel buses, mainly Karrier single-deckers, into service before the first production Thornycroft FC was delivered in November 1928 as the first of an initial order for 10, a further 10 following before the end of 1929. Liverpool was to prove by far the most important customer for the FC; its final order for 40 took the last 15 numbers from the first chassis number series, and then jumped to 19887-911 for the remaining 25 chassis. The whole order was delivered between November 1929 and May 1930, a clear indication of the volume of work that was being handled at that time, although much of the intervening output was in further substantial batches of the light A1 and A2 models.

Liverpool's 60 FC models, all bodied in the Corporation's workshops, formed the largest fleet of Thornycroft six-wheel buses in Britain. Liverpool's last 40 FC buses, placed in service from mid-1930, had WB6 engines, this being the largest of the family of side-valve six-cylinder engines to which the YB6 and ZB6 also belonged. The bore was $4^3/_8$in though the stroke remained at $5^1/_4$in, bringing the swept volume to 7.76 litres, though a power rating of 90bhp was, as usual, on the modest side for an engine of this size by that

Right:
The first production FC Forward six-wheel chassis, number 17421, was for the Liverpool Corporation fleet, the 38-seat body being built in the operator's workshops. The front end of the chassis was very like the BC, including the use of the 6.9-litre ZB6 engine as standard, though with a slightly deeper radiator. From mid-1930, however, Liverpool switched to the larger-bore WB6 engine of 7.76 litres for its later deliveries of the type – this undertaking had the largest municipal fleet of Thornycroft buses. *ATC*

date. It was at about this time that the practice of linking chassis and engine designations began to be used, these vehicles thus being shown in some records as FC/WB6, though the existence of this option was not publicised.

The six-wheel double-deck HC, with ZB6 engine as standard, attracted just one bulk order, for six 56-seat examples with English Electric bodies for Southampton Corporation, dating from the spring of 1929. Two years later there were criticisms from that undertaking of a need for engine overhaul and lack of power; two received WB6 engines, and other modifications followed. It may have been part of the deal that an unsold ex-demonstrator HC passed to this fleet. There were four others, of which two never found buyers and one HC chassis went to Thornycroft (Australia). Of the remaining FC single-deckers, two went to Goodfellow of Hyde, one to New Zealand and one coach to Tysoe of Coventry.

A more fruitful line of six-wheeled development was the JC Forward, a 10-ton goods model with six-cylinder engine. As well as entering a considerably heavier class, it was of up-to-date layout. One prototype was built at that stage, chassis 16980, with ZB6 engine, supplied to the GWR in September 1929. Its general design, and a new heavier-duty rear bogie, held promise for the future, though later versions used larger engines.

A version of the BC Forward suitable for double-deck bodywork had been listed from November 1928 but was not pursued at that date, perhaps because of the decision to concentrate on the market in six-wheel buses, then looking strong, especially for municipal fleets the new two-axle Leyland Titan TD1 was at first being considered as out of line with the view of many of the industry's prominent figures.

Experimental department BC Forward double-deck chassis 19082 was not ready for bodying by Strachans until September 1929. Meanwhile, Leyland had sold over 800 of its very successful TD1 double-decker in the two years from its introduction at the 1927 Show. This made it very difficult for Thornycroft to gain even a small foothold in this fast-growing market with a model which belonged largely to an earlier generation of design, especially as AEC, now again trading under its own name, also had a very effective competitor, the Regent, on general sale from autumn 1929. More specifically, the BC and also the HC six-wheel double-deckers could not match the TD1's low floor level in the lower saloon and the associated ease of entry. The basic problem was that the central position of the rear axle worm

Left:
The HC double-deck version of the six-wheel bus chassis secured only one bulk order; Southampton Corporation took six, on chassis numbered 17434-9, with English Electric 56-seat bodywork of a style typical of the period. They were delivered in March-May 1929, two being seen in the Basingstoke works before dispatch. *Thornycroft Society*

Above:
The typical Thornycroft home-market heavy-duty lorry did not alter greatly in character during the 1920s. The JJ model with MB4 engine was clearly intended as a successor to the J-type, and in this view might almost be mistaken for one, save for the modern-looking wheels and pneumatic tyres. Thomas Wethered & Sons Ltd was also a very traditional type of customer, loyal to the marque over many years. The vehicle shown, KX 1899, dated from February 1929 and was on chassis 18178.
Thornycroft Society

Below:
A heavy-duty six-wheeled forward-control goods model, the JC Forward, was added to the range from 1929. It represented a major step forward in overall design, as well as being the heaviest model built up to then. This prototype with dropside body, on chassis 16980, had a ZB6 engine, though later versions had larger engines. It was supplied to the Great Western Railway in September 1929. *IAL*

casing set a relatively high level for the gangway at this point whereas the offset worm casing of the Titan put it out of the way. This may have been why the Thornycroft designers made the rearmost section of the frame high enough to house a spare wheel, requiring two steps from the ground to reach the rear platform instead of the Titan's one.

Three further BC double-deck models with chassis numbers 19083/4/6 were sold in the spring of 1930 and most of eight further examples built (20316-23) found buyers later that year. In all, four BC double-deckers were supplied to Southampton and four to the Midland General Omnibus Co in 1930, hardly an impressive performance, even though single-deck BC models were doing quite well.

For a year from November 1928, four-cylinder passenger models disappeared from Thornycroft's price lists except for the A2, although in practice UB models continued to be

Below:
A new style of radiator, having a one-piece polished surround, was introduced for the larger passenger models at the November 1929 Olympia Show, this BC Forward, on chassis 18994, having been built for that event – it is recorded as supplied to W. H. Johnson & Sons of King's Lynn in April 1930, but that concern's business was taken over by United Automobile Services Ltd the previous month and this vehicle was not included in the acquired fleet. The two-door 26-seat saloon coach body was built by J. C. Beadle of Dartford. *ATC*

supplied until quite late in 1929. However, in November 1929 the LC models were listed, outwardly like the BC types and having the tidier front-end layout but reintroducing the four-cylinder MB4 engine going back to 1927 to passenger work. Its 6.97-litre swept volume was marginally greater than the 6.90 litres of the six-cylinder ZB6 used in the BC models. The MB4 had been designed to give plenty of torque, though by then quoted as '36/60hp' as opposed to '41/82hp' for the ZB6. An option for the BC and LC ranges also introduced at the 1929 Show was a new polished radiator shell, of similar overall outline to the standard cast version but with a more rounded grille opening and slightly domed front face.

The LC was available as the LC Forward for 32-seat bodywork and as the LC Forward Double-deck seating up to 52 where body weight allowed. They found a following among some municipal customers, Cardiff being noteworthy in taking four LC double-deckers in mid-1930, and SHMD put 24 LC single-deckers in service that year as well as acquiring a further seven together with as a pair of BC models from Goodfellow of Hyde, when its business was taken over in 1935. There were several other independent operators which chose this model, and another, smaller, municipal user was Kilmarnock Corporation, which followed its five UB models of 1927-8 by four LC in 1930, although the undertaking was taken over by the Western SMT company in 1932.

As it turned out, by far the largest user of the LC was the Egyptian General Omnibus Co, formed at the beginning of 1931 to operate buses in Cairo, having been founded in conjunction with an Egyptian associate by Commander F. T. Hare, whose earlier enterprises in Devon and Cornwall had used Thornycroft buses. In this case the British Government gave financial support to Thornycroft for the construction of a fleet of buses. The choice fell on the bonneted LC model

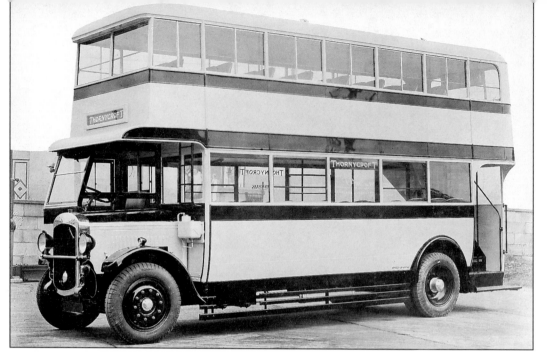

Above:
This BC double-deck demonstrator, 19083, with body by
Strachans, was of low-height layout, with double side
gangways on the upper deck, but the layout of the chassis,
with centrally placed final-drive gears in the rear axle, caused
the overall height to be greater than was possible on other
contemporary chassis. It was demonstrated to Nottingham
Corporation in February 1930 but no sale resulted and it was
sold to Cardiff Corporation in 1932. *Thornycroft Society*

with left-hand drive, an order for 108 chassis being built as
one production run, delivered between December 1930 and
March 1931 even though numbered 20631/2 and 21726-831,
another example of how allocations could 'leapfrog' over
immense ranges issued to other types.

This proved to be the largest single fleet of Thornycroft
buses and in retrospect marked the high point from which a
decline in the passenger side of the business was soon to
become apparent, despite further new models. Later, in
1932, a BC double-deck demonstrator built in 1930 for
Glasgow, 20324, was converted to LC specification, adapted

Above:
The BC Forward model was at about its peak of demand in 1930, and had found favour with municipal operators spread quite widely over Britain. Bournemouth Corporation placed 12 buses of this type on an express bus service providing a faster journey than the trams then serving most of the town – one is seen here at the Square. A further 12 similar buses were ordered soon after their delivery, all 24 having two-door bodies built to the operator's requirements, 18 built by Beadle, four by Strachans and two by J. Martin, a local concern. *IAL*

to run on either petrol or paraffin, and the Glasgow-style Cowieson body rebuilt with the entrance on the right for supply to the EGOC fleet. In all, 160 LC models of all variants were built.

Although larger operators were becoming more likely to place their own orders for bus bodywork, it was still quite common practice for the chassis maker to supply bodied passenger models and Thornycroft continued to use sales names for the types offered. Possibly the best-known of the names used was 'Emerald', though this was far from indicating a specific type, a March 1929 leaflet applying this name to bodies with between 20 and 32 seats on A2 Long, A6, BC and BC Forward models. All were of front-entrance layout but of widely differing detailed design, while another included an 'Enchantress' rear-entrance model and the 'Medway', with doors at the front and rear. In fact, passenger bodywork was subcontracted to various bodybuilders, such as Hall Lewis, Strachan & Brown or Challands Ross, the Nottingham-based agent for the make.

Meanwhile, the BC Forward single-decker had been selling quite briskly, mainly in Britain, though there were several export orders, and this continued until 1931.

Left:
Perhaps the most glamorous of the 1929 Show vehicles was this FC six-wheeler, chassis 17454, exhibited on the Strachans stand, the 32-seat coach body being by that concern – unladen weight was 7 tons 3cwt. It remained in stock until September 1931, when sold to Tysoe's Coventry Transport Ltd, receiving the Coventry registration number VC 9601. The photograph shows it in Nottingham in September 1936 bearing the emblem of BTS Motorways Ltd. *G. H. F. Atkins*

Although the model was superseded by the end of that year, small numbers were built until 1934, taking the total above the 300 mark, the biggest for any purely passenger Thornycroft model. Taking all BC and LC variants, closely related apart from the engines, and including bonneted and double-deck versions, about 540 of this generation of Thornycroft two-axle passenger model were produced.

The LNER followed its initial two BC Forward buses with 12 in November 1928 and 24 in mid-1929, while the GWR took 11 in July 1929. Unfortunately for Thornycroft, the railway companies were by then in the process of giving up their bus fleets in favour of shareholdings in bus companies, mostly belonging to the Tilling and BET combines and, in Scotland, to the SMT group; Thornycroft did not succeed in attracting significant business from these groups though some of their operating companies built up fairly substantial fleets of examples of the make from acquired independent or railway fleets. Quite a large number

Below:
The first of a fleet of 108 buses on the LC normal-control chassis for the Egyptian General Omnibus Co, which proved to be the largest single fleet of Thornycroft buses ever supplied – No 1, on chassis 20630, dated from January 1931. The LC models had the MB4 four-cylinder engine of almost 7-litre capacity but were otherwise very similar to the BC six-cylinder types. The bodywork, with first-class seating at the front and second-class at the rear, was built by Park Royal Coachworks – the unladen weight was just under 5 $^3/_4$ tons. *Colin Morris*

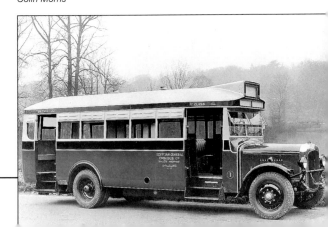

of independent bus or coach operators were Thornycroft
customers, the make having quite a strong following in
Scotland, for example.

The municipal sector proved more fertile ground. In
addition to other examples already mentioned, in 1930
Aberdeen added five BC Forward single-deckers and a
double-deck demonstrator to its 19 A1 models and earlier
types; Bournemouth took 24 BC Forward single-deckers and
Portsmouth six of this model in 1929-30; Gloucester took
four BC Forward in 1929 and in 1932, even though the BC
range was by then obsolete, specified it in normal-control

form for 11 buses in 1932, followed by eight BC Forward in
1933-4; Northampton was another user of the bonneted BC,
with three in 1930.

The 1929-31 period was when Thornycroft bus sales
were at their most extensive; some 14 British
municipalities included examples of the make in their
fleets in 1931. Of these, only SHMD standardised on them
exclusively, but Liverpool had the largest number of
Thornycroft buses, there being five BC Forward models in
addition to the 60 FC six-wheelers, the firm being its
principal supplier in 1930-1.

The railway companies, and especially the Great Western
Railway, continued to be major customers for Thornycroft
goods models. Their need for compact delivery vehicles was
particularly in mind when forward-control versions of the
A1 and A2 were introduced in 1928 and 1929 respectively.
The GWR took 100 of the A1 Forward in 1928-9, these
having solid tyres, by then very unusual on
small models – they had an open-fronted cab
with a small cowl on the driver's side only. By
1929, the specification for an A2 version for
this fleet had pneumatics and a fully enclosed
cab of thoroughly up-to-date specification.
Further batches of these types in forward-
control form were supplied to the GWR, LNER
and Southern Railway fleets in 1930-1.

6. Hard Times in the Early 1930s

The air of success evident in the late 1920s was soon to dissipate, though the depression triggered by the Wall Street crash of autumn 1929 took a year or two to have its full impact. Meanwhile the design team at Basingstoke continued to introduce new models – in one sense, too many.

The great success of the A1 and A2 was the basis for a new series of models introduced in November 1930, allocated the designations A7 to A10, and A12, derived from their predecessors. There was a new engine, the OC4, though even this was based on the previous FB4 and again of side-valve layout, with the bore increased by ¼in to 4in, the swept volume with the unaltered 5in stoke becoming 4.12 litres. The appearance was modernised, with a slightly taller radiator having a slimmer-looking surround, although this latter effect was partly due to the casting of a ribbed pattern in part of the top and bottom tanks.

The best-known of the new types was the 2-ton model, the A10 – when model names were introduced a year later it was called the Bulldog. It was bonneted, with 12ft wheelbase as standard, retaining the main features of the A2. Bearing in mind that the changes amounted to a 'facelift', it is hardly surprising that the first A10 models appeared in what was mainly an A2 stock works order for 100 chassis, 20658-757, mostly delivered from May 1930 to early 1931. Chassis 20741 was an A2, with FB4 engine number 5501, and 20742 was an A10 with OC4 engine number 2, both dating from January 1931, the latter going to Argentina, the

series continuing as A10 to 20757. In fact, in this and some other series, the changeover was not quite as clean-cut as the above suggests, a few OC4 engines going into old-series chassis, for example, and some older-series models continued to appear for a time. There were also A10 Forward and A10 Short (also forward-control) models, plus a low-load version on small wheels for use as a refuse collector.

A similar changeover from A2 Long to the equivalent new-series A12 passenger model with OC4 engine, also occurred in January 1931, the first of the latter being 20892 supplied to Jones Bros (Treharris). That series continued to 20927, Sid Page of Great Yarmouth receiving 12, but the biggest A12 fleet was of 41 left-hand-drive examples (22511-51) for Egyptian General supplied in 1931-2 just before the model was superseded.

The A7 took the load range up slightly, being a 2½-ton model with twin rear wheels. In fact the prototype, chassis

Below:
The railway companies continued to form a major part of Thornycroft's customer base. This JJ Forward dating from 1930-1 was used with trailer on a direct express road service using insulated containers to carry meat from Southampton Docks to the principal towns in Hampshire, Sussex, Dorset and Wiltshire, operated by the Southern Railway. Note the folding starting handle and special radiator with Thornycroft lettering at the foot so as to allow for the nameplate attached to the top tank. *IAL*

Left:
Changing tastes in appearance led to the adoption of this style of radiator for a new generation of A-series models. The vehicle shown was part of a further batch of buses for the Egyptian General Omnibus Co, in this case comprising 41 on A12 chassis and dating from December 1931 to March 1932. *IAL*

Below:
By the time this 2-ton A10 Forward model was built for Coast Lines Ltd, early in 1932, the model name Bulldog had come into use. In this case, the relief colour applied to the chassis, wheels, etc was also used for the parts of the radiator normally painted matt black, giving a quite different effect. *IAL*

21284, could be called the 'father' of the whole series, having OC4 engine number 1 and was delivered to Graham & Morton Ltd in November 1930. Volume production then began with 21458, beginning a run of 48 and including an A7 Forward version – about a year later the type was one of a number to which the model name Speedy was applied, the load rating going up to 3 tons early in 1932. Output of A7 models continued to 1934, with a total of 131.

The A8, later one of the types called the Wolfhound, was a 3-ton six-wheeler, built to a simplified specification, with single-drive and no auxiliary gearbox, but only 18 had been made when output ended in 1933. The A9, a more fully equipped 3½-ton six-wheel model was a successor to the A3 and A5 but again with the OC4 engine – production began in January 1931. Most of these named types were to continue with various modifications under a later model identification system.

It is noteworthy that one of the most successful of this series was at first called the A10 Special, built to the order of Carter Paterson, the specialist in parcel delivery. In effect it was a standard A10 with the FB4 engine from the previous generation of models, of which 129 were built – the LNER also favoured this combination. It became recognised as a model in its own right, becoming the Manly A10/FB4, and remained in production even after the main Bulldog models switched from A10 to new designations as a result of a further engine change early in 1933.

The other A10 variants were built up to July 1934, when production under that designation ceased, and amounted to 507 chassis, quite a creditable figure in the circumstances of the time, but less than a 10th of the combined A1 and A2 figures, although admittedly over a slightly shorter period. Yet the Bulldog was a quality product, well up to accepted contemporary standards. In addition to the depression, it was up against increasingly strong competition; Bedford's 2-ton

model, costing about half as much yet very effective and with a six-cylinder engine, appeared in April 1931.

In the medium to heavier goods range, some of the larger two-axle models at first continued much as built in the late 1920s. The KB, PB, JJ and JJ Forward continued to find buyers, the railway companies and in particular the GWR receiving batches up to 1931. The XB six-wheeler with MB4 engine had sold quite strongly in export markets, a run of 100 being taken up in 1929-30.

There was a move to adopt larger engines for the heavier types of six-wheelers, all still petrol at that stage. First the 10-ton JC six-wheeler, which had begun with the 6.9-litre ZB6, moved up to the 7.76-litre WB6 engine, being built in modest numbers in that form. Six built from mid-1929 to 1930 (18651-6) had the first six engines of this type and, with 10 more built in 1930, went largely to railway fleets, five for the GWR and eight tippers for the LMS.

Then the QC and QC Forward, with 12-ton load rating and a larger engine still, the NC, were announced in

November 1930. As proved often the case in such a project, South African Railways was involved, a JC with NC6 engine number 2 being sent out in July 1930. The NC6 engine, of 11.3-litre capacity, is thought to have been the largest on offer in a production British road vehicle at the time. It had the same $4^3/_4$in bore and $6^1/_2$in stroke as the GB6 engine as used in the Hathi military tractor of 1924, but had a conventional side-valve layout, and was one of a succession of engines of these dimensions used in both marine and vehicle applications over a long period. The power output was quoted as 102bhp, typically modest in relation to its size. The QC chassis design had much in common with the JC, having the capability of traversing rough ground given by the Thornycroft bogie design, but the radiator was rather broader. Such vehicles had appeal in South Africa, Australia and Argentina, though some QCs were sold in Britain.

By late 1931, the QC types had been given the model name Dreadnought, maintaining the link to naval traditions although in this case a battleship, not Thornycroft-built. The numbers constructed were much less than the rather lighter XB achieved, but they laid the foundation for later developments.

The XB itself moved to more powerful engines, beginning with 12 for the Iraq Petroleum Co Ltd, having the 7.76-litre WB6 engine, supplied in July-November 1932; thereafter six-cylinder engines became usual for that model. The number series by then in use, beginning at 19438, was preceded by an example of the EC six-wheeler, originally a passenger type but by then often goods, also

Above:
The A9 was one of a succession of light six-wheel types derived from the A3, having the OC4 engine and 1931-style radiator, seen here with typical military-style body. *Thornycroft Society*

Below:
The QC 12-ton six-wheeler introduced in 1930 was a development from the JC but had the NC6 side-valve petrol engine of 11.3-litre capacity, thought to be the biggest engine offered in a production British commercial vehicle at the time, a larger radiator also being fitted. A demonstrator is seen on test near Newton Poppleford in South Devon. *IAL*

with WB6 engine, in March 1932. This was for Lourenço Marques, also taking six XB/WB6 later in 1932 and again in 1934. By then the model name Amazon was applied to the XB, although destined to be more strongly associated with a later model.

By 1931, the development of diesel engines for road vehicles – in those days generally called oil engines or compression-ignition engines in Britain – was of growing importance. One QC, chassis 21884, is recorded in May 1931 as having a Mercedes-Benz engine for demonstration to Hovis. Although the type of fuel is not given, it seems unlikely at that date to have been anything but a diesel; Hovis was an early user of vehicles so powered. The vehicle was not sold, being later dismantled.

A few makers, in Britain notably the proprietary engine maker, Gardner, as well as AEC and Crossley, by then had oil engines in production, and others were releasing details of examples at a prototype stage, among them Thornycroft. The latter, like Gardner, had an advantage in making engines for marine use, including larger sizes, and the big

NC6 petrol engine formed the basis for early oil engines, though then having a completely different 'top end' with overhead valves.

At a display of oil engines for potential bus use in September 1931, Thornycroft had a six-cylinder prototype shown in a 6½-ton lorry, said to be a JJ. It had a slightly smaller bore size of 4⅝in, bringing the capacity to 10.74 litres; the output quoted was 90bhp at 1,800rpm. Press descriptions did not quote a designation, but this engine seems to have been known as the CI6. Like many early prototype oil engines, it suffered from bearing troubles and was withdrawn.

By 1930, the trolleybus had grown in favour quite strongly, and an agreement was entered into with Brush, one of the leading firms involved in electric traction, to fit Thornycroft chassis with Brush motors and electrical equipment. There were several such agreements between chassis and electrical firms at the time, but this one was unusual in that the vehicles were to be known as Brush-Thornycroft; in the other cases, the chassis maker's name came first.

A prototype based on a stock six-wheel bus chassis, fitted with Brush traction motor and designated HD, was fitted with a Brush 60-seat double-deck body for loan to the Nottingham municipal fleet in December 1930, but the chassis, 22422, was returned after six months. Chassis number 22421, supplied to Derby in August 1933, was also an HD model, but with dimensions, including a shorter bogie wheelbase, compatible with that undertaking's existing fleet of Guy BTX trolleybuses. The only other Brush-Thornycroft sold was a two-axle BD-type single-decker, also built in 1933, with chassis number 22960,

Below:
The setting-up of Brush-Thornycroft Ltd resulted in the production of a prototype chassis, 22422, rebuilt from an existing six-wheel motor bus chassis. It was given the type designation HD and, fitted with Brush electrical equipment and bodywork, supplied to Nottingham Corporation, one of several undertakings then expanding its trolleybus system, in December 1930. It is seen in service as that undertaking's No 28 (TV 3460) in March 1931, but the chassis was returned that summer even though the body was kept and fitted to a new Karrier chassis. *G. H. F. Atkins*

which was demonstrated to and then bought by Bournemouth Corporation. Thus ended what doubtless seemed a promising venture.

New motor bus designs had appeared meanwhile. A revised design of double-decker, the XC, was introduced in May 1931, when five (21863-7) were supplied to Eastern National. The chassis were of more up-to-date pattern than the BC, with a frame permitting a low rear platform and rear axles with offset differential, allowing Strachans to fit low-height bodies. They had MB4 four-cylinder engines initially but are understood to have been re-engined with six-cylinder units quite early in life, one a ZB6 and the others ZD6 units, the latter possibly an overhead-valve version of the former.

Another XC, 21943, was a demonstrator with Strachans body, while 22144 (also initially a demonstrator new in August 1931, but in 1933 sold to Gower Vanguard of Swansea), had a Metro-Cammell body of that firm's then new metal-framed construction, both of these latter having what were recorded as WB6 engines, also with non-standard overhead-valve layout.

The XC acted as an interim design, the frame, chassis layout and overhead-valve engine pointing the way to a new range of passenger models introduced in time for the November 1931 Commercial Motor Show. They were the CD Forward single-decker, given the model name Cygnet, and the DD Forward double-decker, called the Daring. These were both names of early Thornycroft-built Royal Navy destroyers, though as a pair of names for closely related bus models they seemed oddly contrasting in character.

The standard petrol engine for both models was at first the RC6, derived from the special overhead-valve engine fitted to some of the XC buses, having the same bore, stroke and 7.76-litre swept volume as the existing side-valve WB6. Contemporary descriptions refer to the use of duralumin connecting rods and push-rods (the latter a feature also tried briefly by Leyland at that time). From about mid-1933, the engines for these types, though of unchanged design and numbered in the same series, were designated AC6, using conventional materials.

The general layout and appearance were up-to-date, the effect being aided by an elegant new radiator with slim curved surround and a central dividing strip – gradually, this style was adopted on most of the Thornycroft range over the next few years.

The level of refinement given by the smooth-running engine was fully in keeping with the outward impression. In

EASTERN NATIONAL

Above:
In effect, the XC was no more than a stepping stone to a completely new double-deck model, the Daring, type DD. Two of the first five to be built, dating from late 1931, are seen here at the Basingstoke works after repainting from demonstration livery and ready for shipment to Safety Coach Services, of Jersey, in March 1934. The vehicle on the left was numerically the first chassis, 22245, with Ransomes bodywork, which originally ran as CG 617 but was about to be re-registered as J 6992, later running in the Jersey Motor Transport fleet until 1951. The rear-end styling of the bus on the right, 22247, suggests that it may have had Strachans bodywork, of a later style than the ENOC buses on XC chassis. *Colin Morris*

Below:
Another A-series variant was the Speedy A14, introduced in late 1931 and available for both 20-seat passenger and goods applications. It had a new six-cylinder engine, the SC6, of 4.25-litre swept volume and thus smaller than any previous Thornycroft unit of this form. The radiator was of similar style to that adopted for the new Cygnet and Daring. This example was the initial demonstrator, 22552, seen just after return from being bodied by W. L. Thurgood Ltd in July 1932 – it was registered CG 2408 and sold to Mrs A. Horne of Andover in April 1933. *IAL*

The New THORNYCROFT
92 H.P. 4-Cylinder. Type CI.ND4
Compression Ignition Engine.

SPECIFICATION.

ENGINE. Four - cylinder 92 h.p., type C I.ND4 compression ignition engine. 4¼ in. (121⅕ mm.) bore × 6⅛ in. (165 mm.) stroke. Cubic capacity, 461 cu. in. (7,550 c.c.) R.A.C. rating, 36.1 h.p. The engine will start from cold by the electric starter which engages with teeth on the rim of the flywheel. Three-point suspension with spring and **rubber cushion mounting** of the power unit absorbs stresses in the crankcase due to frame distortion, thus a cushioning effect is ensured in the transmission of the torque reaction from the engine to the frame. The trunnions are bolted to vertical faces on the clutch housing, which simplifies removal of the power unit from the chassis. **Either engine or gearbox may be removed independently for overhaul,** leaving the remainder of the power unit in position on the vehicle.

VALVE GEAR. The air and exhaust valves are situated in the cylinder head and operated by push rods and rockers from a single camshaft housed in a tunnel in the cylinder block, and driven from the front of the engine by a **triple roller chain with automatic tensioner.**

CRANKCASE. A deep-section casting of light alloy, exceedingly well ribbed and extending below the centre-line of the crankshaft. Long double-ended nickel-chrome steel bolts pass right through the crankcase, securing the cylinder block at one end and the main bearing caps and steel keeper-plates at the other, thus ensuring extreme rigidity and relieving the crankcase of heavy stresses. The bottom half is easily detachable for the inspection and taking up of the main and big end bearings, etc. The main bearing caps are positively located so that no side

some details, the initial chassis design was just a little 'behind the game', such as in the use of a semi-floating rear axle and single servo brakes, just as triple-servo was coming into favour. By 1934 a revised specification included triple-servo brakes and a fully floating rear axle.

Initial batches of five DD and five CD chassis were put in hand for use as demonstrators and the like, with the first Daring, 22245, completed with Ransomes body for the 1931 Show – it was one of two later sold to Safety Coach Services, Jersey. The first Cygnet, 22250, was sold via

Left:
The first production Thornycroft road transport oil engines had the same cylinder dimensions as the family of petrol engines which had begun with that used in the Hathi tractor. Even in four-cylinder CIND4 form, this gave a capacity of 7.55 litres – a leaflet issued in November 1932 quoted a claimed output of 95bhp at 1,800rpm, but it was quite a heavy unit at 17¾cwt with gearbox. *ATC*

Below:
Most of the earlier Cygnet CD models went to independent operators, among them J. Foster & Sons of Otterburn, Northumberland, which took delivery of this example with Beadle bodywork on chassis 22953, registered JR 523, in May 1933 – the livery was a distinctive orange, black and cream. The author still recalls its smooth running on a very agreeable journey over the operator's route of 30 miles or so from Newcastle in early postwar days. *Colin Morris*

Thurgood, which bodied it as a 32-seat bus, to People's Motor Services Ltd of Ware early in 1932, registered JH 1587. It became one of a dozen Thornycroft buses which passed with that business to London Transport in November 1933, this one later being sold to Salopia Saloon Coaches of Whitchurch, Salop, joining two Cygnets already in that then largely Thornycroft fleet.

There was also renewed interest in smaller six-cylinder models and it may have been the impact of such vehicles from Bedford and also the Leyland Cub that led to the introduction of the SC6 engine, announced in late 1931, this being an overhead-valve unit of $3^{1}/_{2}$in bore, $4^{1}/_{2}$in stroke and 4.26-litre capacity. Its applications were the Tartar A13, another light six-wheeler, for on-road use, of which only five were built, the Speedy A14 two-axle model, offered for both 20-seat passenger and goods applications, and, on paper, the Wolfhound A15 six-wheeler, though none of this last was completed. A prototype A14 was 21506, with SC6 engine number 3, sold to R. Hamilton & Son in August 1932, and a run of 10 A14 passenger mostly found homes with British independent fleets, though two went to China Motor Bus Co in Hong Kong – in all, 18 A14 were built. Another passenger type with the SC6 engine was the Ardent AD 26-seat model introduced for the November 1931 Show – briefly, once again the entire listed passenger range was six-cylinder.

In 1932, a pair of production oil engines was introduced, reverting to the $4^{3}/_{4}$in x $6^{1}/_{2}$in cylinder size. The CIND6 (sometimes quoted as CINC6) was a six-cylinder version with the familiar 11.3-litre swept volume, while the CINC4 or CIND4 was the equivalent four-cylinder engine, of 7.55 litres. These were built in limited numbers for use in goods models, as mentioned later, but the CIND6 was too big and heavy for passenger work and the CIND4 was not listed for any production bus model, though in 1934 SHMD converted 12 of its LC-type single-deckers with what were described as 82hp Thornycroft four-cylinder oil engines, evidently the CIND4.

Sales of both Cygnet and Daring proved disappointingly slow, the model appearing just as the depression was deepening, though further modest stock works orders for 10 of each model were built in 1932-3. Dundee Corporation

was the largest customer at that stage, with five Daring models (22501-5) having Metro-Cammell's new standard style of body in 1932, two similar vehicles also being among the last buses supplied to the Perth municipal fleet.

The first Daring chassis of this batch, 22500, was built as a demonstrator with a Gardner 6LW oil engine of 8.4-litre capacity, and is believed to have been the first Thornycroft bus fitted with an oil engine from new. The body order went to J. C. Beadle of Dartford, which bodied quite a number of Thornycroft bus or coach models in this period. It was registered CG 3025 in December 1932 and sent to the SHMD fleet in December 1932 – the first, on chassis 23127. The 8.4-litre 6LW, developing 102bhp at 1,700rpm, had ample torque and was well suited to the hilly area around Stalybridge – and was purchased by that undertaking in August 1933, prompting further orders for the type.

Southampton took four petrol-engined Daring buses with Park Royal bodies in 1933. However, interest in oil engines was growing and Aberdeen took four Daring models with locally built Walker bodywork so powered in 1933, two having engines by Beardmore, a Glasgow maker somewhat favoured in Scotland for a time, and two had Gardner engines, recorded in Thornycroft records as 6LW. By early 1933 an export bonneted version was added to the range, this being the Charger, type ED, although two buses for the São Paulo Railway built on CD Normal chassis were completed that April.

The decision to adopt model names for the whole Thornycroft range put into effect at about the end of 1931 was followed by a period when the identification of the various models became very confusing. Not only were there

numerous types – the firm claiming the widest range in the world – and indeed far more than could be justified in terms of economic production, but the names were sometimes applied inconsistently and seemingly without much regard for suitability. In some cases they were even switched from model to model, hardly giving potential buyers the chance to become familiar with them and thus losing the intended benefit from a sales viewpoint.

Thus, in early 1932, the KD/MB4, a 5-ton bonneted model with the big 6.97-litre four-cylinder petrol engine as standard and having a taller version of the Bulldog-style radiator, was called the Strenuous. Yet this name was also applied to a completely different low-loading forward-control 5-ton model derived from the BC Forward passenger chassis and designated LD/ZB6 – the Distillers Co Ltd had one in 1933, by which date the standard engine had become the AC6. In April 1932, the name Sturdy was applied to the PC/HB4, a 4-ton bonneted model of similar appearance to

The general adoption of model names from late 1931 led to a period of some confusion, as they were by no means always applied consistently. In sales leaflets issued early in 1932, the 5-ton KD/MB4 was called the Strenuous; one of them showed this vehicle registered OU 9316, evidently a demonstrator. The design was largely in the mould of late 1920s models, mildly modernised by a new radiator and servo four-wheel brakes. In February 1933, a new leaflet for the KD/MB4 showed this same vehicle, but the model name had become the Sturdy, hitherto applied to a rather similar-looking but lighter PC/HB4. *ATC*

A completely different Strenuous was in reality a goods version of the BC Forward, though designated LD/ZB6 Forward in this manifestation, shown in a leaflet dated April 1932; the registration VX 9569 indicates issue early in 1931. Low-loading goods models derived from passenger equivalents were briefly fashionable around that time. *ATC*

Above:
For a time in the earlier 1930s the Taurus became the main bonneted goods model in the 6-6³/₄ -ton class, the layout with the front axle set back being quite widely favoured for a time. This mid-1932 example for Johnson Bros of Runcorn was used on the leaflet for the JD/AC6 Long version. *ATC*

Below:
Among the more apt model names was Iron Duke, applied to the YC model designed as a heavy-duty tipper. This vehicle, registered OY 1088 in Croydon in mid-1931, may have been the prototype, 21053, known to have been built for Hall & Co Ltd, which ran a large fleet of tippers. *ATC*

the Strenuous KD but with the medium-sized 5.42-litre four-cylinder engine and built in modest numbers in 1931-3. But by April 1933, the KD/MB4 5-ton model switched from the Strenuous name and itself became a Sturdy, though none of these models was to become anywhere near as well known as a later group of types given the Sturdy name from late 1935. The KD, under whichever name, was in production on a small scale until 1934, later examples including some with CIND4 engines.

Briefly, there was somewhat similar confusion at the heavier-duty end of the two-axle goods range, with some early examples of a heavier-duty chassis in the 6½-ton class given the name Jupiter in 1932, although the basic design became much better-known as the Taurus. This was type JD, of which an early example, 21050, with ZB6 engine, was completed for demonstration in May 1931. This design took up what was, for a time, quite a popular concept among commercial vehicle makers, in being a 'snouted' bonneted model with the front axle set back so as to leave most of the bonnet projecting ahead of it, the idea being to increase overall load capacity by taking some loading off the rear axle, also giving a smaller turning circle and very good engine access. Such a layout was particularly favoured in some export markets and left-hand-drive examples were quite common.

Records of early examples sometimes refer to the type as JD4 or JD6, the former with MB4 and the latter with WB6, but soon the range of engines became much wider, with the CIND4 oil engine quite a common choice, as well as some examples with the ZB6 or, later, the AC6 petrol units. The Gardner 4LW was a further option.

Basically very similar to the Taurus was the Iron Duke, type YC, with a similar range of engines, evidently aimed especially at the heavy-duty tipper market. One with an MB4 engine, 21053, possibly the prototype, was built for Hall & Co Ltd, the sand and gravel merchant, in May

1931 and is probably that registered OY 1088 shown on a leaflet for the model. Two demonstrators had the CIND4 but one example is noteworthy in having a Mercedes-Benz OM5 engine.

There were similar complications to the six-wheel goods range. As already mentioned, the QC was given the name Dreadnought by November 1931 and continued in production as a 10-11-ton model in 1933, by then having an overhead-valve version of the 11.3-litre six-cylinder petrol engine, the ND6, as standard and the CIND6 as the oil engine option. However, what had been the QC Forward now became the QD, and there was also a QE. Outwardly almost identical was the Jumbo 11-12-ton model listed by 1933, again with ND6 or CIND6 engine options, the TD version being bonneted and the TE with forward-control. At least two QCs are known to have been rebuilt as TE models.

The XB bonneted six-wheeled model that had been in production since 1927 continued as the Amazon, rated at 6 tons on good roads but intended largely for use on rougher surfaces. From 1933 the range of engines offered included the AC6 and the CIND4 as well as the MB4, by then rare, and there was one each with Gardner 5LW and 6LW, the latter for the SAR fleet. Broadly similar and with the same range of standard engines, but simplified by the omission of the auxiliary gearbox, was the Mastiff SD bonneted six-wheeler rated at 7½ tons with no reference to off-road use – a batch of five was built in 1933.

Below:
The XB had graduated somewhat from its original 1927 design. This example, coupled to a semi-trailer with a representative load of pipes, was on chassis 19439, one of 12 dating from July 1932 supplied to the Iraq Petroleum Co Ltd. They had WB6 petrol engines and were on large-section tyres to suit operation on soft sand. IPC was to remain a regular customer for many years. *Thornycroft Society*

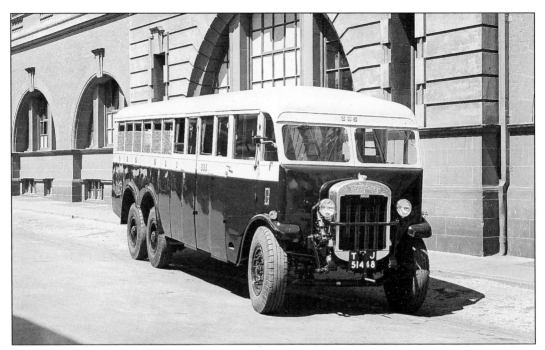

Above left:
A contrasting development of the XB was the South African Railways combined passenger and goods version. In 1934 seven chassis with the AC6 petrol engine were supplied, and SAR had developed its 'tri-compartment' body to produce a functional design suitable for use where roads were unsuitable for conventional passenger models. By that date the Amazon type name appeared in small lettering at the top of the radiator grille. *Thornycroft Society*

Left:
One of the stranger model names was that of the Manly 2-ton chassis, applied to a special version of the A10 with FB4 engine supplied to Carter Paterson, the express cartage specialist. This one, registered ALM 123, earned fame by carrying the luggage of car drivers taking part in the International Alpine Trial in the summer of 1933. Its role was to travel ahead of the competitors, often via the same Alpine passes. *IAL*

Above:
Light six-wheel models were also offered in several forms. The Wolfhound A8, with OC4 engine, had a 4-ton load rating, only one rear axle being driven, and there was no auxiliary gearbox. This example for Boot's, registered TV 4846, dated from mid-1931 and was thus almost certainly an A8, but its photograph was used for the leaflet describing the Wolfhound in its GE/GD4-form overhead-valve engine as offered from 1933. *ATC*

Below:
The Tartar was the double-drive equivalent to the Wolfhound, suited to off-road work. This photograph of one supplied to Scremerston Coal Co Ltd, a small colliery a few miles south of Berwick, was used on the leaflet issued in 1933 for the LE/GD4 forward-control version. The older style of radiator, as used on A-class models of the 1920s, tended to be retained for such types – military Tartar models were still so equipped in 1939. *ATC*

Lighter six-wheelers still were the Wolfhound GE bonneted and HE forward-control 4-ton and Tartar KE bonneted and LE forward-control 3-ton models offered from February 1933. The Tartar models were capable of off-road use, with auxiliary gearbox, and were offered with the SC6 4.26-litre six-cylinder engine first seen in the A13 to A15 models in 1931, this engine being favoured War Office examples, or a new overhead-valve four-cylinder unit, the GD4, reverting to the $3^3/_4$in by 5in dimensions of the much-loved FB4 used in the original A1 etc.

The main application for the GD4 was as power unit for most of the new range of two-axle models also offered from February 1933 to replace the later A-series types, though in most cases closely related to them in much the same way as were the Tartar and Wolfhound six-wheelers. As indicated by these latter as quoted above, there was an alphabetic pattern of type codes with E as the second letter. Thus there were the Bulldog $2^1/_2$-ton CE and DE and Beauty $3^1/_2$-ton EE and FE, the first of each pair respectively bonneted and the second forward-control.

There was a further complication in that the EE became a Speedy when fitted with the SC6 six-cylinder engine. The Ardent passenger model became the EE Long (bonneted) and FE Long (forward-control), now with the GD4 engine, and the Lightning name was revived for a six-cylinder version of the EE Long, using the SC6 engine.

Such proliferation of types makes the tracing of production batches more complex, especially as old-series and new-series models would be lumped together where basically similar. Thus the run of 150 Bulldog and related chassis from 23148 to 23331 was made up of 50 DE/GD4, 25 CE/GD4, 50 A10 (1 with OC4 and 49 with FB4, these thus of the Manly type, including 20 for Carter Paterson) and 25 CE Long (mostly GD4 but with one Dorman 4 JUR), mostly delivered during 1933, though the DE forward-control batch ran until November 1934.

Up to a point – it is rarely possible to be dogmatic about Thornycroft variations in this era – the newer bonneted models had a radiator of similar style to the Cygnet, with the forward-control versions at this stage retaining the style as used on Bulldog models or, if basically 'military', even the A1/A2 type. The as yet missing AE and BE were to follow later in 1933.

Below:
Amid the complexities of model names and type letters in the early 1930s, the use of 'Speedy' for the EE chassis when fitted with the SC6 six-cylinder engine seemed appropriate for this example equipped as a fire engine by Simonis, to which Thornycroft acted as chassis builder. It was on chassis 23642, supplied via the South African agents Robertson & Moss to Durban Fire Department in September 1933.
Thornycroft Society

7. Changes in Direction

Despite the variety of models being offered – 40 distinct types were quoted in 1932 – orders for vehicles had diminished in the early 1930s and workers had to be laid off, this extending to staff, even those that remained suffering a 10% pay cut. The firm returned losses from 1932 to 1936, surviving on the strength of its reserves built up in more successful days.

After the Herbert Engineering Co, makers of HE cars, went out of business in 1931, its factory at Caversham, Reading, was acquired. It took over the production of engines for river-going and other smaller sizes of craft, hitherto carried out at the Basingstoke works. Construction of boats continued at Hampton-on-Thames. Possibly the most famous of these was *Miss England* built in 1932 for Lord Wakefield, which succeeded in breaking the world water-speed record by reaching 119.81mph on Loch Lomond – she had two Rolls-Royce aero engines giving a total of 4,720bhp.

Naval construction was still at a modest level in the early 1930s, though two destroyers were built in 1932-3, one being the second to bear the name *Daring*, also in use for the double-deck bus model then current. Two more were built in 1936 and other work was obtained. Among notable Woolston-built vessels of that period were the paddle-steamer *Gracie Fields* and the luxurious motor yacht *Shemara*, the latter for Sir Bernard Docker of the BSA empire.

There were resignations in this period among the management, the most dramatic being that of Tom Thornycroft in May 1934, both from his position as General Manager at Basingstoke and as a Thornycroft Director. The financial position of the firm had worsened in 1932 and 1933, adverse results on the vehicle-building side of the business being the major factor. An independent accountancy firm's report made recommendations and it is known that there were differences of opinion between Tom and the other directors on future policy. Clearly he was in a difficult position, but the whole commercial vehicle industry had experienced a sharp drop in trade.

Tom Thornycroft was a charismatic figure, well regarded within the works as well as beyond, and perhaps the most adventurous of the family members – he was to continue his interest in the development and racing of motor boats and yachts until shortly before he died at the age of 74 in June 1955. His departure from the firm probably hastened the decline in the bus and coach side of the business – although existing models continued for a while and some prototypes of new ones were built, no new models primarily designed for bus work were put into volume production thereafter.

The Basingstoke works passed through an uneasy period, although efforts to attract business continued. Agreements with specialists had been set up, with Simonis to build fire engines, Eagle for refuse collectors (for which the low-loading chassis were designated AA) and Ransomes for a crane model, but none of these resulted in large-scale orders. It was recognised that the CIND4 and CIND6 oil engines were unsuitable for other than heavy-duty models and in mid-1933 the Gardner 4LW engine of 5.6-litre size and the Dorman-Ricardo 4JUR four-cylinder 4.2-litre engine were offered for Thornycroft models. The latter was available in the Beauty EE 3^1/$_2$-ton model and slightly later the Steadfast name reappeared for the FE 4-ton type. Another model of

Above:

In 1933, the Dorman 4JUR oil engine was offered in the FE chassis, the model name being switched in such cases from Beauty to Steadfast. This FE/4JUR Long was supplied that year to C. T. Clark of Wrexham for the transport of milk churns. A 'Dorman-Ricardo Diesel' badge was carried on the dash, just behind the radiator cap. *IAL*

this era having a Dorman-Ricardo engine, in this case the 4DS unit, was the Bullfinch 3-ton type CE and DE – in effect a Bulldog 3-tonner with this engine option.

The most imposing new model to appear at the November 1933 Show was the Stag 10-12-ton six-wheeler, type XE, using the AC6 7.7-litre petrol engine or, in a few cases, the CIND6 11.3-litre oil engine, looking much more modern than the Dreadnought QC and Jumbo TE it replaced. It had an unusually deep version of the slim-surround central-strip radiator set with a distinct rearward slope, the cab front being similarly inclined.

The Stag was presented at the time as a 'lightweight' model, but this was more a matter of a token response to new goods vehicle taxation provisions based on unladen weight. The main source of weight-saving was a single-drive rear bogie but even so, the unladen chassis weight came out at over 5½ tons, appreciably heavier than competitors' models

designed from scratch to meet the new requirements. At first sales were encouraging, with an order for 40 of the XE/AC6 supplied to Metropolitan Transport Supply Co, a company providing transport for the International Stores chain of grocer shops, completed by mid-1934, but only 30 more had been built when the model ceased to be offered in Britain by 1937; smaller numbers were built mainly for export until 1938.

More important was a new 2-ton model, the Handy, especially in its BE forward-control form, although the AE bonneted version inherited the role of earlier 2-ton models, also being built in quite large numbers. Both types reverted to the simple FB4 side-valve 3.62-litre engine first seen in the A1 nine years earlier, but the BE had a new cab designed to lift off by crane for maintenance in a matter of minutes – it had a rather crude version of the centre-strip grille. The short wheelbase gave a car-like 36ft turning circle and the LNER and GWR promptly responded with orders for 31 and 84 respectively, all delivered by early 1934. Its name was among the most apt of the range, and examples were bought for local delivery work by a variety of users.

New engines were also being introduced. The AC4 was a four-cylinder version of the AC6 petrol engine with the same 4⅜in bore and 5½in stroke, giving 5.1-litre swept volume, and was promptly offered as an option in the Cygnet, among the first going to Tom Tappin Ltd of Wallingford in March 1934. Soon it became quite widely used for goods, and later even more so for military models.

The DC6 provided an oil engine option directly interchangeable with the AC6, though its cylinder dimensions were different, with 4⅛in bore and 6in stroke, this giving 7.88 litres and thus being marginally larger in swept volume than the AC6's 7.76 litres. It was advanced at that date in having a one-piece casting including the cylinders and crankcase, and provided the basis for a very successful family of engines, even though this was not evident at first.

Thornycroft's injection system of the time could be described as a cross between direct and indirect injection, as the fuel was injected downwards into the cylinders across an air cell. No heater plugs were needed and the claimed output of 98bhp at 2,100rpm was impressive. However, contemporary road test reports remarked on some emission

Right:

The Stag 10-12-ton six-wheeler, model XE, introduced in 1933, was of unmistakable appearance, with its deep sloping radiator. Single tyres of 13.50-20 size were standard on the rear bogie. The model was no longer listed when this example on chassis 29701, one of a pair with AC6/1 petrol engine, was built in mid-1938 for use by the Courage brewery concern, then based in Alton. The unladen weight was 6 tons 16cwt 3qr, hardly in the 'lightweight' category sometimes claimed for the model. *IAL*

of black smoke when accelerating. Also introduced at that time was a 5.25-litre DC4 four-cylinder of the same cylinder size.

The first production DC6 engine, No 1, was fitted in a Daring DD (24067) for Southampton Corporation and placed in service in February 1934, though it seems that the chassis may have been built initially with an AC6, this perhaps accounting for unfounded reports that it had an AEC engine, but it is significant that the undertaking's next bus orders were for Guy Arab buses with 5LW engines, in 1934-5. The SHMD fleet also took delivery of five DD models (24290-4) in the winter of 1933-4, the first two with DC6 engines and three with Gardner 6LW units, but the DC6 units were soon replaced by 6LWs, this latter becoming the

Above:
Certainly not Thornycroft's most elegant model, but a much-needed source of business in a difficult period, was the forward-control BE version of the Handy, one of the more apt model names. The Great Western Railway had ordered 84 of the type as soon as it was announced, two being seen here at the Paddington Goods Depot shortly after they entered service early in 1934. *IAL*

Below:
The bonneted Handy, type AE, was of more traditional style. These three, supplied to Coast Lines Ltd, Leith, and registered in Edinburgh as AFS 447-9, dated from mid-1936 and were unusual in having cabs and bodywork by Park Royal Coachworks Ltd. *ATC*

Above:
Adding to the sense of variety, this furniture van delivered to Alfred Bell (Newcastle) Ltd in December 1935 was on a Cygnet CD/AC4 passenger chassis, number 24337, with four-cylinder petrol engine and oak-framed body by REAL, of Ealing – it was numbered 65 (CTN 428). Bell ran a regular Newcastle-London service with a fleet of vans in a green and red livery. *IAL*

standard for what was to prove the largest fleet of the model, amounting to 16 by the time the last were delivered in 1936. With Northern Counties 48-seat bodies, except on the initial ex-demonstrator, they were sturdy yet quite light vehicles with exhilarating hill-climbing capabilities, even if rather noisy internally.

A Charger ED/DC6 with left-hand drive was built for Athens and a few DC6 engines were fitted in Stag models, but the 6LW was chosen for a Charger for South Africa and a Daring for Australia in 1934, though there were two Cygnet CD/DC4 and one CD/DC6 for Australia in 1935.

More significantly, the Gardner 4LW was chosen for 10 Cygnet models for the Kowloon Motor Bus Co (1933) Ltd, operating in the mainland areas of Hong Kong, which were shipped in mid-1934. They were the first oil-engined buses supplied to that colony and established a preference for Gardner engines that was to continue long after the Thornycroft era. A further 10 CD/4LW were built in 1935, but they were for the China Motor Bus Co Ltd, operating on Hong Kong Island. In 1936, SHMD chose the 5LW engine for its one delivery of eight Cygnet single-deckers.

Thornycroft continued its active interest in articulated vehicles and, in November 1933, bonneted Handy AE/FB4, Beauty EE/GD4 and Speedy EE/SC6 tractors rated at 4, 5 and 6 tons were being offered alongside a Steadfast EE/4JUR with Dorman engine and Taurus JD/AC6 and JD/CIND4 types rated at 10 tons. In September 1934, the bonneted Handy AE/FB4 Long was offered in 20-seat

passenger form, early users including Tillingbourne Valley Services with a Thurgood-bodied example; in 1936, the Caledonian Omnibus Co Ltd took two with Brush bodies.

What was to prove one of Thornycroft's best-known model names appeared in October 1934, with the announcement of the first Trusty, type PE, designed to suit the then new goods vehicle taxation system. It was a forward-control two-axle model with a load rating of 7½-8 tons within the 12 tons gross limit for two-axle models then in force. It had a front axle set far enough back for the driver to enter via a step ahead of the front mudguard and had the slim-shell well-rounded radiator with central strip that was to remain standard for heavier Thornycroft models until the war years. A range of engines was offered, with the AC4, DC4, AC6 and DC6 as the main types, although the CIND4 was also offered for a time and there were Gardner 4LW and 5LW options. Chassis design was conventional, with straight parallel frame, four-speed gearbox, overhead worm rear axle and triple-servo brakes – there were alternative 12ft 8in or 15ft 3in wheelbases.

Above left:
The introduction of the six-cylinder 7.88-litre DC6 oil engine early in 1934 was an important step towards wider adoption of this form of power, as it could be fitted in any model having the AC6 petrol engine as standard. It proved not to have been entirely satisfactory in its original form, but was later developed with a Ricardo-designed combustion chamber as the DC6/1 and then as the direct-injection DC6/2 as well as being the basis of the NR6 used from 1944. *ATC*

Left:
Southampton Corporation took two Daring DD petrol-engined double-deckers, on chassis 22506/7, in January 1933, one of which is seen here, followed by two more in July. In February 1934 a further example, outwardly similar and having the same style of Park Royal body, entered service but this had DC6 engine number 1, thus being the first bus with a Thornycroft oil engine. *IAL*

Above:
Early bonneted equivalents to the forward-control Cygnet single-decker were of type CD, but a longer-wheelbase version was type ED, given the model name Charger. These five, on chassis 24296-300, were of type ED/AC6/LH with six-cylinder petrol engines, supplied via Thornycroft (Egypt) to the Ramleh Electric Railway in November 1934. The bodywork was by Brush. *IAL*

At first production was on a small scale – two early examples were 25049/50 of 1935, which had the AC4 5.17-litre petrol engine, although publicity put some emphasis on the DC4 oil engine. Both of these units fitted within the compact cab length but the extra length of the six-cylinder engines was accommodated by positioning the radiator nearly a foot further forward, with a short projecting bonnet. From late 1935, the DC4/1 engine with the Ricardo indirect injection system superseded the DC4, giving an increase of power to 85bhp at 2,200rpm.

The DC6/1, with similar changes and giving up to 125bhp, was also announced, though the changeover in that case seems to have gone into production slightly later. There were also detailed revisions to the similar-sized petrol engines, causing them to become AC4/1 and AC6/1 by 1937.

The Trusty OE bonneted model, with the same alternatives in specification, was announced in October 1935, inheriting the proportions of the Taurus which it replaced. Heavy-duty PD forward-control and UD bonneted versions followed in time for the 1936 Scottish Show. A UD tractor version, offered only with six-cylinder engines to operate at up to 22 tons gross, followed in 1937.

Meanwhile, by 1935, although the firm was still suffering occasional spells of short-time working, the trade position was improving and, in addition, there were signs of changes in policy aimed at developing a simpler and more rational model range. By then the Basingstoke works was in the charge of R. C. Charles, who took a direct interest in the early design stages of new models.

The first order for new buses placed by the Kowloon Motor Bus Co (1933) Ltd, Hong Kong, was for 10 Cygnet CD chassis with Gardner 4LW oil engines. Numbered 24794-803, they were shipped in June/July 1934 and bodied locally to a style clearly influenced by British practice, one being seen when newly completed. The larger rear hub as compared to earlier models of this series indicates a fully floating rear axle. Hong Kong became an important market for the Cygnet, in that case always with 4LW engine. *IAL*

Above:
The Trusty range was at first confined to two-axle models, the first to appear, in October 1934, being the PE forward-control 7½-8-ton type, offered with a wide range of engines. The set-back front axle continued to be favoured, allowing easy entry to the cab via rear-hinged doors. This example for Redpath, Brown & Co Ltd, registered in Lanarkshire as AVD 227, dated from spring 1939, showing the compact form of cab fitted on models with four-cylinder engines. *IAL*

Larger-scale production batches of the Trusty began to appear from spring 1936, with an initial 50 of the forward-control PE and PD types (25658-707) and 50 bonneted OE and UD (26171-220), both being completed by 1937. A further 200 numbers were allocated for Trusty models from 26973, mostly taken up on completed vehicles by the end of 1939. In addition, a series for UD tractors began at 27748 at the beginning of 1938 and 40 of these were built by 1940. Thus, in round figures, prewar Trusty output, all two-axle, amounted to about 350, a modest showing in an important market.

In October 1937, one bonneted OE type (27131) was built with a Gardner 5LW engine, this being a van supplied to Portals Ltd, a special-purpose paper maker based at Laverstoke Mills, a few miles from Basingstoke, a small-scale but regular customer. This option thereafter caught on to some degree and 10 of the 172 PE models were Gardner-powered (seven with 5LW engines and three with 4LW). There were three PD models with the 5LW and eight Gardner-engined UD models.

Although a more standardised range was in hand from 1935, it took a little while for the complexities of the model ranges to cease growing further, perhaps influenced by a need to use up stocks of parts. The formula which had resulted in the Handy 2-ton models was extended by mid-1935 to the 2½ to 3½-ton range with the introduction of the Dandy CF bonneted and DF forward-control models. These, and also by then the Handy AE and BE models, used the improved FB4/1 petrol engine, still basically the simple 3.62-litre side-valve design first seen in the A1 but now revised by the adoption of a Ricardo-designed cylinder head. The forward-control Dandy DF version had the same readily detachable cab concept of the Handy BE but had the

Top:
Thornycroft, having pioneered articulated goods vehicles, maintained its interest in the subject. One of three Bulldog models supplied to the London & North Eastern Railway early in 1934 is seen in this view. *IAL*

Above:
The bonneted Handy became available in passenger form from September 1934. This example, an AE Long/FB4/1, was chassis number 25368, for Percival Bros, of Gunnerside, near Richmond, Yorkshire. It was registered VN 8391 and delivered in March 1936 – the bodywork, by Waveney of Lowestoft, suited the model particularly well. *ATC*

Left:
The bonneted Trusty was introduced in model OE form a year later, this being the first of the series, on chassis 26171, supplied to Alfred Button & Sons of Uxbridge in March 1936 and registered DMP 506. As with so many early Trusty models, it had an AC4 petrol engine. *IAL*

Above:
The Trusty UD bonneted model was added for export and other heavy-duty purposes in 1936, this UD/AC4 being one of a pair, 26182/3, delivered to R. H. Neal & Co Ltd in November 1936 as a basis for that company's 3-ton cranes and supplied to the Anglo-Iranian Oil Co Ltd. *IAL*

'proper' style of radiator grille as by then used for the bulk of the range, including the BE type itself.

Passenger versions of the CF and DF were also produced, but these were called Dainty, and the Caledonian Omnibus Co Ltd was again a customer for small Thornycroft buses, with three CF in 1937 and two in 1938, with Brush 20-seat bodywork, the vehicles looking much the same as the pair of 1936 Handy AE models already in the fleet. The bonneted GC was of similar appearance but slightly larger, being called Ardent if four-cylinder but Lightning if having the SC6 six-cylinder engine. The Dainty DF forward-control model, capable of seating up to 26, was based on the standard goods chassis with its quite high-set full-fronted cab layout, having little more than softer springs to distinguish it as a passenger model. About two dozen were sold to independent operators in 1936-7, one being Venture Ltd of Basingstoke, which took delivery of one with Wadham Bros 26-seat body in July 1936, its last new Thornycroft.

Success with a New Sturdy

The most important development in late 1935 was the introduction of a new Sturdy range. This extended the concept of the smaller goods models, with their simple yet good-quality engineering, to the 4/5-ton class. The TC4 engine was another side-valve four-cylinder unit derived from the FB4 concept, this time with $3^7/8$in bore but still with 5in stroke, giving a swept volume of 3.865 litres and developing 62bhp at 2,400rpm. There were dry cylinder liners and the high-mounted distributor helped accessibility.

The chassis had an overhead worm-drive rear axle and servo brakes, and there was a simpler new straight-sided radiator without the centre strip, having the small Thornycroft nameplate projecting slightly into the grille area at the top. The front mudguards swept lower than previously, projecting beyond the dash panels of forward-control models and being joined by a panel below the radiator. The overall appearance was tidy and functional, effectively conveying the character of the model. The first version to appear was the ZE/TC4 with forward-control and alternative wheelbases, soon followed by equivalent bonneted YE/TC4 models. Unlike previous bonneted types, these retained the same positioning of the radiator as the forward-control versions, helping to give quite a compact layout. To carry the full 4-5-ton load, they generally weighed about 3 tons with platform bodywork, but $3^1/2$-4-ton versions with

Above:
The Dandy, introduced in 1935, applied the same formula as the Handy to models in the 3-ton class. However, the DF forward-control version was given the standard style of centre-strip radiator, as shown here on a van for The Gas Light & Coke Co Ltd, then responsible for gas supplies in the London area and using 'Mr Therm' for a series of sales campaigns. The 'DF 1936' shown on the registration plate suggests it was a 1935 Show exhibit. *IAL*

Below:
It seems to have been realised that the 'proper' radiator of the Dandy DF looked better than the version on the original Handy BE design of 1933, so the same version was adopted for later Handy BE models. This example for the LNER dated from early 1936. *IAL*

Above:
The complexities of the Thornycroft range continued in the mid-1930s. The Lightning name was revived for the GC model when fitted with the SC6 engine, of 4.25-litre capacity. The GC chassis took the Ardent model name if fitted with the FB4/2 engine. This GC/SC6, chassis 24690, with Wadham 26-seat body, is thought to have been ordered by Logan & Courtier, who traded as 'Parma Violet' from premises in Boscombe, taken over by Hants & Dorset Motor Services Ltd in September 1935, though it was delivered direct to the latter as S532 (BEL 607) the previous month. *ATC*

Below:
The winding down of the passenger range in 1936 left only the Dainty, with FB4/1 engine, as a catalogued model. The forward-control DF version seen here made no concessions to contemporary ideas on passenger vehicle appearance, the front-end with high-mounted radiator designed for a full-width goods vehicle cab being retained. The example shown, chassis 25720, was supplied to W. L. Silcox of Pembroke Dock as its No 9 (BDE 96) in January 1936. *ATC*

smaller-section tyres and other lightweight features could be brought below $2^{1}/_{2}$ tons unladen weight limit and were thus eligible to run legally at up to 30mph under the regulations of the day instead of the 20mph applicable to heavier goods models. There were also low-loading models with smaller wheels for use as refuse collectors etc, but the basic designations did not change for any of these variations.

The chassis price of £415 to £440 was still well above the £250 or so of a Bedford or Ford 3-ton model at that time but, at the full load rating, catered for a market then beyond the range of the mass producers. It was very competitive as judged against comparable Albion, Dennis or Guy models. An initial short batch of perhaps five ZE models began at 25544, but demand was strong enough from the beginning for the first major runs to cover 200 ZEs beginning at 25821, and then 100 of the bonneted YE. All were delivered in about a year from mid-1936 and about 1,200 had been built up to the outbreak of war in 1939, the YE accounting for about a quarter of these. Together with accelerating military

vehicle demand, the Basingstoke works became busier than it had been since about 1930, helping the company as a whole to return to profitability.

In 1936 it was announced that Thornycroft was to cease offering full-sized passenger models. In one sense this was understandable, as sales had continued to be very modest, though perhaps in turn reflected a lack of enthusiasm for this line of business. Southampton Corporation returned to the Daring chassis for four Park Royal-bodied 56-seat double-deckers in 1936-7, these being the last of the DD model to be built. Significantly, they had Gardner 5LW engines; four Leyland Titan models were purchased at the same time, this

Left:
The refuse collector market had been the subject of a collaborative arrangement with the Eagle Engineering concern of Warwick since the late 1920s. The Sturdy ZE/TC4 followed previous practice in being made available with smaller wheels to give a lower loading level for this purpose, although the change to 29in x 7in size was less extreme than evident previously. Seen here is one of a pair with Eagle rear-loading bodies built in 1938 for use in Poplar. *IAL*

type becoming standard in that fleet until 1939. At SHMD, from 1937 the choice stayed with Gardner engines but in Daimler chassis.

However, Kowloon Motor Bus of Hong Kong followed its earlier Cygnet CD/4LW buses with 20 more in 1938, and China Motor Bus followed five Cygnet supplied in 1936-7 with six in 1938 and a final four in 1940. There was also an upsurge in interest in the six-cylinder petrol-engined version of this model on the part of South African Railways – an order for 10 was placed in 1937 and a further 21 were supplied in 1937-8, these latter CD/AC6/1. Together, these export orders gave what could be described as a 'posthumous' upsurge of production after the ending of home-market deliveries. Ironically, the cut-off of home-market availability had caused Venture Ltd, Tom Thornycroft's bus-operating business in Basingstoke, to set up a remarkable exercise whereby other manufacturers drew lots for what was the firm's largest order for new buses; AEC was the winner, supplying six Regent double-deckers in March 1937.

By the time the official list of standard home-market models offered in Autumn 1937 was compiled, the Thornycroft goods range comprised the Handy AE and BE, the Dandy CF and DF, these all with the FB4/1 engine, the Sturdy YE and ZE, with the TC4 engine, and the Trusty OE

and PE, plus the UD as a tractive unit, with the choice of AC4/1 or AC6/1 petrol engines and DC4/1 or DC6 diesels. Much of the mystifying complexity of only two or three years earlier had gone, with four basic types, even though amply covering the 2-ton to 8-ton range.

On the other hand, it was remarkable that no six or eight-wheeled models were offered for home-market users at that stage, especially in view of Thornycroft's earlier strong involvement in multi-wheeled vehicle development and growing output of such vehicles by competitors. The Thornycroft passenger range had shrunk to the Dainty CF and DF, plus a new passenger version of the forward-control Sturdy, called the Beautyride ZF/TC4 for 26-seat bodywork, first displayed at the 1937 Show, with a front end like the goods ZE although the chassis differed from that model in having a lower frame level, swept up over the axles, and an underslung worm rear axle. In total 19 were sold, of which nine went to an Argentinean operator, CITA, these having Perkins Panther diesel engines.

Although six-wheelers were not listed for the home market, important new export models of this type began deliveries in 1936-7. They used the name Amazon previously applied to the venerable XB design dating back to 1927, but were fresh models owing more to the Trusty range in their layout and appearance, even though some of the mechanical features were inherited from the XB and were also found on the Stag XE.

The new bonneted Amazon, type WF, had a projecting bonnet akin to the Trusty OE or UD, while the forward-control XF had a front end similar to that of the six-cylinder forward-control Trusty models. The standard engines were the AC6/1 petrol engine or the DC6 oil engine, with four-speed main gearbox and two-speed auxiliary option, with triple-servo brakes.

The official load rating was a modest 5 to 7 tons, but that reflected their cross-country capabilities. A Super Amazon, rated at 8 tons and on larger tyres, was offered from late

Left:
The Amazon, type WF, had close affinity to the bonneted Trusty models in its front-end design. This early example with four-wheel trailer, a WF/DC6, chassis 26475, was exported to Geminiani Roldan & Cia, of Bell Ville, Argentina in July 1937. Note the Thornycroft nameplate on the bonnet side and the 'El Coloso' lettering on the cab. *IAL*

Above:
Surprisingly, in view of the decision to withdraw from the manufacture of full-sized models specifically designed as buses, the largest Thornycroft exhibit at the Commercial Motor Show held at Earls Court, London, in November 1937 was a glamorous-looking coach, even though based on the new Amazon WF six-wheel goods chassis. It was one of three on WF/6LW chassis for Iraq State Railways and the Park Royal body had luxurious armchair seating for only 20 passengers, with a full-height luggage compartment at the rear. *IAL*

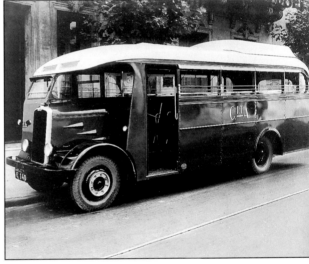

Right:
British vehicles and ideas were much respected in Argentina at that time and although the standard Beautyride passenger version of the Sturdy ZF was built with goods-type full-width dash, this example, one of nine with Perkins Panther engines supplied to CITA of Mendoza in October-November 1938, had a half-cab front-end. The body, though built by Catita, a Buenos Aires concern, showed evidence of being influenced by Duple bodies supplied on Leyland Tiger buses already in service. *IAL*

1938. The XF was mainly a South African Railways model, 77, all with AC6 petrol engines, being supplied to that fleet out of the 80 built in 1936-8. The first major order for the WF was for 14 with Gardner 6LW engines for the Iraq State Railways, mainly lorries, but three had luxurious Park Royal 20-seat coach bodies.

Another six-wheel range which continued in production was the Tartar, listed by 1938 as export 4-4½-ton models KF (bonneted) and LF (forward-control), with AC4/1 and DC4/1 engine options; a few had Gardner 4LW engines. This was increasingly a military series, with examples supplied to both the British Army and the governments of countries such as India, Sudan and Egypt.

The rationalisation at the smaller end of the standard goods range was taken a step further with the introduction at the Scottish Show in November 1938 of the Nippy range of 2- and 3-ton models, bringing to an end the complex AE, BE, CF and DF series, as well as the venerable FB4 engine, of which over 7,500 had been made since its introduction in 1924.

The new Nippy models had the 3.86-litre TC4 petrol engine already in production for the Sturdy, with basically similar if simplified and lighter chassis design, the brakes not having a servo. The main model was the HF/TC4, with forward control, though there was also a GF/TC4 bonneted type. A 20-seat passenger version of the HF, this time with

straight frame, was available, and Tillingbourne received one (28857) with Wadham body. The general appearance was broadly similar to that of the Sturdy, with the radiator of conventional outline though having a more elaborate and somewhat controversial grille.

The choice of name was apt, for the type was quite a lively performer by the standards of the time; 'Nippy' was also in those days the nickname of the waitresses employed by J. Lyons at its numerous teashops dotted all over London, and famed for their swift service – this might not have been coincidental, as Lyons had many Thornycrofts in its fleet of vans. Demand for the Nippy models proved quite lively from the start, with about 200 built in the first year.

In November 1938, a new three-axle goods model to carry up to 10 tons was exhibited at the Scottish Show, this time of the twin-steering type, by then being offered by ERF, Foden and Leyland to cater for a need falling between conventional two- and three-axle models. The name Dreadnought was revived for it, though its design features belonged to the Trusty family. It used the Gardner 5LW engine as standard, perhaps because of its modest weight. This model had not gone into production before the outbreak of war in September 1939 and it is understood that the prototype was dismantled, though 10 were later released to operators.

Also announced in November 1938 was a new, smaller oil engine, the MD6, intended for the Sturdy range, though noteworthy as having six cylinders. The bore size of $3^1/2$in was the same as the SC6 petrol engine but the stroke was reduced to $4^1/8$in, giving a swept volume of 3.9 litres, and its construction, with an integral cylinder block and crankcase having seven main bearings, indicated that it was a fresh design. An output of 70bhp was claimed at unspecified speed. Here too, the onset of war stopped progress, though nine Sturdy ZE models with MD6 engines were built in 1943 as a stepping stone to later developments. Oil engines were still uncommon for vehicles of this size range, though a small proportion of prewar Sturdy models was built with the Gardner 4LK, a four-cylinder engine of 3.8-litre capacity, and a very few with Perkins engines.

Top:
The last major new model introduction before the war years was of the Nippy, the 3-ton example shown being on the forward-control HF/TC4 chassis. It was supplied to W. B. Wardlaw & Sons Ltd of Windygates, Fife. *IAL*

Above:
The Nippy HF/TC4 Long was available in passenger form and Tillingbourne Valley Services took delivery of this example on chassis 28857, with Waveney 20-seat body, registered HPL 265, in the spring of 1939. The radiator casing was conventional, if lacking a distinctive Thornycroft outline, but the patterned grille proved controversial. *Colin Morris*

Right:
There were many examples of users' loyalty to the marque. This 1939 scene shows three Trusty PE models of 1936-8 and two Sturdy ZE of 1938-9, with a third just visible, all operated by Steward & Patteson Ltd of Norwich, brewer of Norfolk Beers. The projecting bonnets of the PE models indicate that they were six-cylinder models. *IAL*

8. War Again – but with More Technology

The outbreak of war on 3 September 1939 again found Thornycroft in the front line of military production although, contrary to the common impression, a substantial build-up had begun about two years earlier, influenced by growing concern about Germany's policies under Nazi rule. The Admiralty had put a new 'Tribal' class of 16 larger destroyers of 1,870 tons in hand in 1937. Thornycroft built two at Woolston, delivered in 1938, and two of a slightly smaller type followed.

The firm had continued as a major supplier of Army vehicles throughout the interwar years and, even though numbers had been small, the good relationship meant that it was one of the first to be given the larger contracts, of which deliveries began from early 1938. The death of R. C. Charles in August 1939 left the position of Managing Director of the Basingstoke works vacant and R. F. Newman, who had been assistant to the works manager in the late 1920s, was appointed. By then Charles Burton had joined the company as Chief Designer, having previously held that post with Gilford, and continued until the late 1950s.

In 1939, the typical Army lorry was a forward-control six-wheeler with a four-cylinder petrol engine, still retaining the

Below:
Production of military vehicles was stepped up from 1938 under the threat of a war. This scene shows deliveries of Sturdy ZS searchlight lorries for the week ending 15 January 1939 when chassis numbers 29481-93 were supplied from a run of 377 such vehicles. *Thornycroft Society*

canvas-topped cab, and the Thornycroft Tartar had played an important part in its development. As is apt to happen with vehicles intended for cross-country work, the model had evolved into a slightly heavier-duty range with the WO, of which a prototype (26402) was built in mid-1937 and 470 were delivered in 1938-9. It was followed by the WOF, destined to be by far the best-known of the Tartar models, with a massive run of 1,140, taking the numbers 31169-32308, delivered between January 1940 and June 1941. The AC4/1 petrol engine of 5.17 litres, as used in many prewar Trusty models, was adopted for these types – broadly similar vehicles were being built by several makers, the Army favouring petrol engines to standardise fuel supplies.

Some needs were met by normal production models of civilian types, and substantial numbers of Sturdy or Nippy models were taken from stock or impressed from civilian users in the early weeks of the war. However, many of what outwardly looked like conventional bonneted Sturdy models were built to a searchlight lorry specification, type ZS, in which the space under the bonnet was occupied by a large 15kW dynamo supplying the power for the searchlight and driven directly from the front of the engine, which was within the cab, much as in a forward-control model. A prototype, 25939, was built in 1937 as part of the first standard ZE model production programme, and an initial 150 were built in 1938, followed by 377, then 550, all supplied by the end of 1939, as anti-aircraft defences were strengthened. A further 614 followed in 1940-1 and further ZS models were built in smaller batches later, some being used for other purposes.

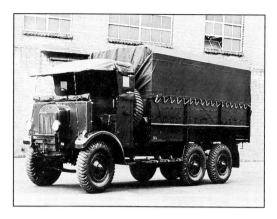

Official sources quote a total of 1,576 searchlight lorries among Thornycroft's war production.

A quite different adaptation of an existing model was the use of the bonneted Amazon WF, hitherto an export type, as a basis for a mobile crane for use by the Royal Air Force. The Amazon chassis was well suited to this by reason of its layout, and the cross-country capability not only allowed these vehicles to reach aircraft which made forced or crash landings but also to be used for tasks such as changing engines where bombers were dispersed beyond the hard standing of concrete runways. The military Amazon WF chassis was fitted with large-section tyres, but the earlier examples otherwise retained the general look of the model as introduced in 1937, the AC6 six-cylinder petrol engine being favoured until almost the end of war production.

An initial batch of 10 was delivered to Coles, the Sunderland crane maker, in March-September 1939, followed by 50 in service by May 1940, and from then output was virtually continuous, with larger production runs of 150, 250 and 160 delivered between then and the end of 1942. By then the RAF bomber fleet was operating from bases in most parts of Britain and the Thornycroft-Coles cranes became a familiar sight, a few being supplied for Navy use.

In the period from September 1939 to the summer of 1940, a semblance of normal output was kept going on a reduced scale. Among the more noteworthy batches in hand until December 1939 was one of 99 Trusty UD tractor units with AC6 engines for the Republic of China, which had already received 200 Sturdy YE models earlier in the year. In the aftermath of the fall of France to the German army in

Above:
The traditional style of Army lorry standard in the earlier part of the war was of this pattern, with six wheels, forward control and cab with folding hood. This Tartar was of the WOF/DC4/2 type and thus had the diesel engine first put into production for such vehicles from October 1941. *Thornycroft Society*

Below:
The Amazon, in bonneted WF/AC6 form, provided the basis for a mobile crane for use by the Royal Air Force. The cross-country capabilities of an early example were being tested here on an example bearing Hampshire (and hence doubtless Thornycroft) trade plates in a scene which may well have been on Chobham Common. The ability to reach crashed or force-landed aircraft over such terrain was of particular value. *Hampshire County Museum Service*

Above:
The ZS/TC4 looked very like the civilian-bonneted version of the Sturdy, but the engine was actually under a cover in the cab, the bonnet being occupied by the dynamo providing power for an anti-aircraft searchlight, which could thus be set up wherever desired and quite independently of public electricity supply. *Thornycroft Society*

mid-1940, virtually the whole of Britain's productive capacity was mobilised. However, Thornycroft was one of very few makers allowed to continue limited production of civilian models under Government control and allocation, in this case mostly standard petrol Sturdy and Nippy types. For example, 350 Sturdy ZE went to essential civilian users in the two years from September 1940, of which six had Gardner 4LK engines. In 1943, nine ZE with the very rare MD6 oil engine announced in 1939 were released. Some 57 Trusty PE models, all with AC4/1 petrol engines, were delivered between October 1939 and December 1942. In all, nearly 2,000 vehicles were supplied to civilian users under the wartime allocation scheme of 1940-5.

Another military product was a four-wheel-drive vehicle. Soon after the war began Thornycroft was chosen to develop a new 3-ton model of this type, the requirement being that it was to be capable of climbing up to a 1 in 2 gradient, operating on desert sand for long periods and be capable of running at up to 40mph on a normal road. The desert requirement was to prove important when the British Army became involved in the North African campaign that same year.

Above:
The bonnet of a ZS searchlight lorry open, showing the 15kW 100V generator, directly driven from the front of the engine, the latter housed within the cab in the manner of a forward-control model. The radiator was also set back, though the normal outer casing was retained, complete with top tank and filler, connected by hose. The dynamo shown was made by the Electric Construction Co Ltd of Wolverhampton, which produced equipment for Guy trolleybuses prewar. *IAL*

Left:
Civilian deliveries continued fairly normally in the early
months of the war. These Southern Railway Nippy HF models
have received the obligatory white paint on bumpers and
mudguard edges but not the headlamp masks compulsory for
wartime use. They had bodies built to SR specification by
Cunard of Wembley. *IAL*

Below left:
Typical of many civilian vehicles running by about 1941 was
this Sturdy operated by the British Oxygen Co Ltd.
Unvarnished liveries, usually grey, were adopted partly as
being less easily visible from the air and partly because
of supply shortages. The registration FYY 3
suggests that it was new early in 1940. *IAL*

Right:
Large numbers of women took jobs in the
Basingstoke works as in other factories in wartime,
though this lady, looking as though she was all set to
enjoy driving a Sturdy ZE to the bodybuilders, may
have been a full-time delivery driver. *IAL*

Below:
Deliveries to civilian users included a production run of 50
Trusty PE models, mostly dispatched in 1940 to 1942. All had
AC4/1 petrol engines, possibly because that unit was then in
large-scale production for Tartar and Nubian military vehicles.
This example for The Distillers Co Ltd has both headlamps
masked, as adopted by 1942. *IAL*

Above:
The Nubian TF with an AC4/1 petrol engine went into production in February 1941 and was built in large numbers thereafter. The War Office's ideas on military vehicle design had swung towards four-wheel-drive, resulting in a relatively high build – the characteristic appearance is conveyed by this fine model. Although designed when austerity was part of the national mood, there was a hint of the Stag in the sloping radiator and cab front. *Hampshire County Museum Service*

The resulting TF model was given the name Nubian, another Navy name adopted for a Thornycroft vehicle type and given to a succession of types thereafter. One example (30993) was supplied to the War Office in June 1940 and volume deliveries began in February 1941 – in all, 3,824 of the wartime Nubian 4x4 model were supplied, including a large batch for the RAF.

Mounting the AC4/1 petrol engine above a driven front axle inevitably resulted in a higher build than a type with conventional non-driven cranked front axle beam. However, this was regarded as not unwelcome in a vehicle also intended to be able to drive straight up the beach from a landing craft, helping to keep vulnerable items such as the ignition system out of reach of the water. Even so, the Nubian had an unusually tall build in its wartime form. By that stage, instructions had been given to simplify radiator designs for ease of production and the original Nubian had a very plain style, with rectangular mesh grille. The Amazon radiator also changed to a more austere style.

On the Nippy and Sturdy models for sale to civilian users from about 1943, a completely new style of grille was incorporated into the cab front panel, again with a 'utility' facing. In this case, the surround ran counter to most wartime practice in having a curved profile. It was a steel pressing, with the outline reproducing the prewar Sturdy style. Its profile required the cab front also to have the same degree of curvature, at a time when cab outlines were often becoming more austere and square-cut, except when made from existing pressings. The standard Thornycroft cab had the windscreen panels in a vee formation and with the profile below them following the grille curvature, the overall outline was quite stylish, especially by the post-1942 'utility' standards which imposed austere lines on bus body construction. By contrast, the later military Sturdy normal-control models with front-mounted generator acquired a singularly ugly box-like bonnet, wider than standard and with plain rectangular grille.

The wartime output of vehicles of Thornycroft designs was much larger in total than had been produced during the

Top right:
From about the beginning of 1943, civilian Sturdy and Nippy chassis were supplied with a grille to be incorporated in the cab front. Although cab designs varied, the grille's curved profile dictated a similar line for the cab, giving a more modern look. This Sturdy 6-ton model seen outside the local dealers was the 36th Thornycroft supplied to Longton Transport Ltd. It seems likely to have been 37722, an early example of the ZE with the improved ER4 engine, delivered in March 1943. *IAL*

Right:
Challands Ross & Co Ltd, the Nottingham Thornycroft dealers, had a capable bodybuilding department and made good use of the scope given by the new type of grille to produce a stylish appearance to this Nippy 3-ton van built for W. E. Saxby (Nottingham) Ltd. The chassis, an HF/ER4, was 33573, delivered in June 1943. *IAL*

entire 1930s – in all, some 13,000 wheeled vehicles were
supplied to the armed forces, yet that was by no means all.
The Bren gun carrier was a light tracked vehicle developed
by the War Department and powered by a Ford V8 petrol
engine, Thornycroft being one of the first concerns to put the
type into production – output continued through the war
period, a total of 8,230 being built. A fully amphibious
vehicle, the Terrapin, powered by a pair of Ford V8 engines,
was also developed, one being completed in June 1943
(42605), but production was allocated to Morris Commercial.
An improved Mark II version was under development in
1945, with four more prototypes (45805-8) but the end of
the war brought the project to a close.

Machining for the Woolston shipyard had been carried out
at Basingstoke in peacetime, and was to continue in postwar
days, but larger-scale involvement in maritime work at
Basingstoke included the manufacture of depth-charge
throwers and parts for torpedoes, of which 15,000 sets were
produced. In addition, there were 1,700 sets of 17-pounder
and 670 sets of 2-pounder guns.

As in the 1914-18 war, construction of destroyers was
expanded, tending to be spread around more shipyards than
in peacetime, although at Thornycroft's Woolston yard 12
were launched between 1940 and 1945, to which can be
added two under construction for Brazil in 1939 also taken
into Royal Navy service. There were also five escort sloops.
but the largest ship built for the Navy during the war was the
cruiser minelayer *Latona*, launched in August 1940, a 2,650-
ton ship with a speed of 40 knots. She was to have only a
brief career, being sunk by Italian aircraft off the coast of
Libya a little over a year later. The Hampton boatyard built
over 50 motor torpedo boats and motor launches. Both yards
were also involved in the production of landing craft.

Sir John E. Thornycroft remained in charge of the
business through the war years, his title in 1946 being
Governing Director and Chairman, but by then he was 74
and many duties were shared by three Joint Managing
Directors, among whom a third John Thornycroft was
effectively heir-apparent – this was Lieutenant-Commander
J. W. Thornycroft RN (Retired), who had served in the 1914-18
war on a Thornycroft-built destroyer, and held a master's
certificate. Effectively, R. F. Newman ran the Basingstoke
works subject to the Board's policy guidance and was to
continue in this role until 1961.

Technical Advances in Wartime

Even though the urgent demand in wartime was for
production of the various types of vehicle and other
products, engineering development did not cease. An

important figure in this period was W. S. Dack, who had joined Thornycroft in 1937 as Experimental Engineer; previously he had been Assistant Experimental Engineer with AEC. He was given quite a free hand, and produced a revised double-deck bus chassis design, reflecting renewed interest in this market. One prototype chassis, quoted as type DD/5LW and with chassis number 35131, had been completed by January 1940. The war stopped further work on the project, the chassis being used as a 'journey vehicle', to quote Thornycroft's phrase for a works transport lorry. It had a very different appearance from the earlier Daring DD models, with a new style of radiator.

Of broader value was the development of a direct-injection version of the Thornycroft oil engine, the work being based on the DC4 and DC6. It will be recalled that Thornycroft had adopted the Ricardo indirect-injection system from 1935. This had been favoured by and developed in conjunction with AEC in 1931, giving increased power, smooth running at speed, and greater reliability than some of the early designs, but was not able to match the fuel economy of the better direct-injection systems; starting from

Below:
Among the wartime products of the Thornycroft boat yard at Hampton-on-Thames was a batch of air-sea rescue launches, each powered by two Thornycroft RY/12 engines developing 650hp and giving a speed of just under 25 knots. The vessel shown was one of nine dating from 1942. At Basingstoke, Sydney Dack was pursuing a plan to modify captured Daimler-Benz aero engines to increase the speed, and although this was not pursued, it inspired development of petrol-injection postwar. *IAL*

cold was also not always easy. Both these latter factors were of importance for possible military use and Sydney Dack brought knowledge of AEC's development of a direct-injection system, adopted as standard there soon after he left. That used a toroidal cavity in the piston, being covered by patent, but for Thornycroft he was able to arrive at a design using a cavity of near-hemispherical contour with a more rounded central tip, giving good results. A patent application made in July 1942 was granted the following June. Examples were running just before the war and it was intended that the engine was to become available for the Nubian, though in the event the petrol unit remained standard for wartime output of that model.

Early production engines with direct injection were four-cylinder units derived from the DC4/1 and designated DC4/2, being used in later batches of the Tartar WOF, from October 1941. Further developments were made to ensure reliable starting under extreme cold, an auxiliary ether system allowing DC4/2 engines so fitted to start without difficulty at -40°F.

A more comprehensive wartime redesign led to the introduction of the NR6 engine, having the same $4\frac{1}{8}$in by 6in cylinder dimensions and 7.88-litre swept volume as the DC6 but with direct injection, dry cylinder liners and divided cylinder heads. This was adopted for later examples of the Amazon mobile crane – engine number 2 of this type was fitted to WF chassis 39698 delivered in April 1943 and the NR6 was adopted for production Amazon models just as the war ended, becoming standard for almost all Thornycroft's larger home market models postwar.

Also initially in the experimental category were further developments in multi-wheeled goods models, although 10

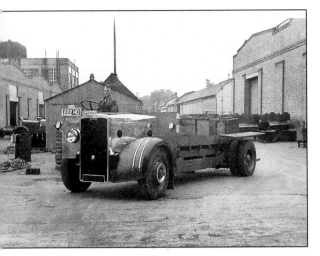

The prototype double-deck bus chassis built in 1939-40 under the supervision of Sydney Dack and numbered 35131 is seen in the works yard at Basingstoke. Although quoted as of type DD and having the then familiar Gardner 5LW engine, it was of new design – Dack had been much involved with bus development in his previous post with AEC. The style of radiator was to remain unique, though echoed in slightly more angular form in the few postwar DG and SG passenger models. The nearside mudguard was a rubber moulding, a concept briefly quite popular at the time. The rear hub shape suggests that the axle was a Kirkstall product. *ATC*

sets of parts for the NF/5LW twin-steering six-wheeler, similar to the 1938 Show example exhibited as the Dreadnought model, were assembled into completed vehicles and delivered to operators in the early wartime period, the last in November 1941. A prototype eight-wheeler with Gardner 6LW engine, chassis 29730, was put in hand in April 1940, but was overtaken by more urgent wartime needs, not being completed until later. Designated PF/6LW, it was delivered to Motor Sales (Longton) Ltd in July 1945, just after the war in Europe had ended.

Although eight-wheeled Trusty PF models were to figure prominently in postwar production, a Gardner-engined option was not then offered, so this particular combination remained unique. Yet the choice of Gardner engines for these vehicles and the prototype double-decker suggests that, as matters stood in 1939-40, this make of engine was intended to be available at least as an option. By that date, almost all British operators of vehicles in these classes wanted direct-injection engines and, as indicated, work was in hand to fulfil that need with Thornycroft engines.

Perhaps the most remarkable wartime project in which Thornycroft, in the person of Sydney Dack, was involved was a plan to use Daimler-Benz DB601 aero engines taken from Luftwaffe aircraft shot down over Britain to give better performance from Thornycroft-built RAF high-speed air-sea rescue launches. The DB601 engine was roughly equivalent to the Rolls-Royce Merlin as then widely use in RAF aircraft, at that time both giving about 1,000bhp, and this would have been enough to produce a significant improvement in performance compared to the 700bhp given by the existing Thornycroft marine engine built in the Reading works for use in the RAF boats.

The pressures of the aerial Battle of Britain meant that every available Merlin engine was needed for the defending fighter aircraft. Yet the safe recovery of pilots who had to bale out over the English Channel was, if anything, even more important, as trained pilots were less easily replaced than aircraft. The Germans also sent out high-speed launches into the Channel, so speed was important. It seems remarkable that there were enough undamaged engines to make such a scheme seem practical, quite apart from the problems of being able to keep them in good order. The idea was dropped but it gave Sydney Dack considerable respect for the DB601's petrol-injection system – at that date the Merlin used a conventional carburettor.

Beattie's Bakeries Ltd of Glasgow was another regular Thornycroft customer and this fleet of Sturdy bread vans is seen outside the premises of Croft Bodybuilding & Engineering Ltd, a concern which grew in prominence during the war years. *IAL*

9. Postwar Prosperity

Past and possible future customers were asked for views on their postwar vehicle needs via the regional sales offices as early as the winter of 1942-3. The Nippy and Sturdy ranges received general approval, save that some thought the Sturdy a bit underpowered. This time, few of the ex-military vehicle types were suitable for civilian use, the notable exception being the Amazon with Coles crane. After six war years when new vehicles had been scarce, order books soon filled across the whole commercial vehicle industry.

The continued output of the Nippy and Sturdy for civilian users throughout the war gave these types a good basis for expansion. From January 1943, the prewar TC4 petrol engine had given way to the mildly revised ER4 as standard for these smaller models, but the latter retained the side-valve layout and 3.865-litre capacity as used previously, better breathing increasing the power output to 68bhp at 2,600rpm. The Nippy, now sold as a 3-ton model, thus became the HF/ER4, available in standard, long and tractor versions, the last-mentioned with Scammell coupling to allow use with Mechanical Horse semi-trailers – the Great Western Railway was a major user.

The Sturdy forward-control 5-6-ton ZE/ER4 was almost directly comparable to the 1937 ZE/TC4 version, but the price as quoted in 1946 of £810 to £865 was virtually double that asked prewar, a reflection of wartime inflation. A new option, increasing the chassis price by £195 and available from early 1945, was the TR6 indirect-injection oil engine. It was a six-cylinder unit, based on the MD6 design announced in 1938, of which the few sold in 1943 thus acted as a pre-production run. The bore size was slightly increased to $3^9/_{16}$in and, with the same $4^1/_8$in stroke, gave a swept volume of 4.042 litres, with a 67bhp output. Postwar forward-control Nippy and Sturdy models at first continued with the style of cab introduced in wartime, but the less common bonneted models still had the prewar type of radiator.

The first postwar Sturdy ZE production run, delivered to users from May 1945, was split as 250 with the new TR6 oil engine and 250 with the ER4 petrol engines, both being used up by spring 1946, though sales of the diesel version

Below:
Output of the lighter models continued seamlessly into the early postwar years. This Sturdy ZE for the Carborundum Co Ltd of Manchester, dating from late 1945, had the wire-mesh – or, to be more precise, expanded-metal – grille and absence of plated parts standard from wartime. *IAL*

Left:
The introduction of a Thornycroft oil engine option for the Sturdy as delivered from May 1945 helped to secure sales at a time when the large-volume makers of vehicles in its weight range had yet to follow suit. The illustration shows TR6 engine number 2. *IAL*

Below left:
The 'Sturdy Diesel' badge on the radiator grille draws attention to the type of engine in this ZE/TR6, chassis number 45850, delivered to R. G. Bowerman Ltd of Taunton in May 1946. The grille itself by then had vertical slats and a chromium-plated surround. In the year since this engine was introduced about 300 Sturdy models so fitted had entered service. *IAL*

Bottom:
The Great Western Railway continued to be a major user of Thornycroft vehicles, in this case an early postwar Nippy HF/ER4 tractor with Scammell semi-trailer in use at Slough station. The GWR road vehicle department preferred to keep cab design simple, to make repair of the minor damage which tended to be suffered on local delivery work easier, and mounted the curved-profile grille on a plinth. The cab was made by James Whitson & Co of West Drayton, well known as a coach bodybuilder. *IAL*

Right:
The Amazon WF8/NR6 found new roles, this example, registered in London as HYE 858, being one of 24 tippers in the fleet of Sir Robert McAlpine & Sons Ltd placed in service in 1947. *IAL*

Below right:
On the other side of the world, this Amazon was supplied to the South Australia Engineering & Water Supply Department, the semi-trailer being built in Victoria. *IAL*

Above:
Among the first Trusty PF/NR6 models to be supplied, in
January 1947, were two, 46314/5, for Blomfield Transport Ltd
of London E14. It seems that advantage was taken of the
delivery run on trade plates to take some crated items to
London docks. *IAL*

gradually drew ahead – over 4,000 postwar Sturdy models
had been built by 1950. The Nippy remained available only
in petrol form, with a little over 2,000 sold during that period.

In the immediate postwar era, the first heavy-duty model
to be offered was the Amazon, by then designated WF8 and
in the form as produced at the end of the wartime contract,
with NR6 oil engine and the 'utility' radiator. Most, though
not all, went to export markets, beginning at the end of 1945.
Users included various oil companies in both the Middle
East and South America as well as contractors, with various
types of body, including cranes by Steels. The postwar
chassis number series began at 46409, some 589 being
delivered, the last few in 1953.

The preceding run of 100 numbers, starting at 46309, had
been reserved for the initial postwar Trusty, at first offered
only in eight-wheeled form, in contrast to prewar, when this
model was built only as a four-wheeler. Deliveries began in
September 1946, this first batch being completed early in
1948; 120 more had followed by 1952. The PF/NR6 had an
18ft 4in wheelbase and was rated at 14-15 tons within the
22-ton gross weight then applicable, with a double-drive rear
bogie having two-spring suspension – all four axles were
bought complete from Kirkstall. The 7.88-litre NR6 engine

gave 100bhp at 1,800rpm, and by 1948 a five-speed gearbox
had become standard. Advanced features for that period
were the air-pressure brakes and their provision on all
wheels – most competitive eight-wheelers then omitted
brakes on the second steered axle. A new style of radiator
had some affinity to the style first seen on the Sturdy from
1935, but a new feature was the large 'T' emblem on the
grille, this latter soon to be adopted for almost all models.

The Trusty range was extended by the addition of the two-
axle VF and three-axle RF models, of which specifications
were issued in 1947, although initial output was on a modest
scale, the first RF models not appearing until 1949. The VF
chassis differed from the equivalent prewar PE in not having
the set-back front axle, the position of this axle in relation to
the frame and cab now being common between VF, RF and
PF types. No twin-steer model to succeed the 1938/40
Dreadnought NF was produced.

The NR6 engine, or from 1949 the NR6/MV with
modifications to give better breathing, was standard for all
of this generation of Trusty models. The prewar Gardner
engine option was not revived, despite several requests for it
to continue reported in the wartime survey, though the slow
deliveries Gardner could offer due to strong demand may
have been a factor. Surprisingly, 11 VF models built in 1948-9
for brewery fleets had AC4/1 four-cylinder petrol engines.

In Britain, petrol engines were generally regarded as
obsolete for the heavier-duty types of commercial vehicle by
the end of the war, but this was not yet so in some export
markets, notably South Africa. Sydney Dack put his
knowledge of the possibilities of petrol injection, gained

'Petrol injection' is a phrase apt to slip off a modern car salesman's tongue, yet Thornycroft had a vehicle so powered running very successfully over half a century ago. This cross-section of the NR6/PI engine shows how the injector for each cylinder was placed just behind the inlet valve, spraying fuel into the flow of air into the cylinder as the valve opened – the spark plug is shown in dotted lines. *Thornycroft Society*

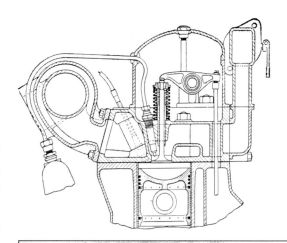

from wartime study of Daimler-Benz aero engines, into modifying an NR6 engine to this system, believed to be the first petrol-injection road vehicle engine, designated NR6/PI. Retaining the 7.88-litre swept volume, it gave 150bhp and increased torque. Comparison of one in a PF eight-wheeler (chassis 46310) with a standard PF/NR6 in April 1947 showed much livelier and very refined performance, including smooth and effortless cruising at 40mph, leaving the diesel well behind.

However, fuel consumption, though better than for a conventional petrol engine, was still markedly inferior to

Right:
The Trusty RF/NR6 forward-control six-wheeler was a comparatively rare type, this example on chassis 51078 being completed as a mobile workshop for the Rhodesian Railways and seen here before being shipped in March 1950. *IAL*

Below:
The Trusty VF/NR6 could be used with drawbar trailer, as in the case of this example with standard cab and dropside body of Permanite Ltd of London E3. *IAL*

diesel standards and this ruled out the system for adoption in Britain. Sydney Dack left the company in 1947 to take a post with the White Motor Co in the United States, but his successor Ken Martlew did some further study, and Amazon chassis 46718 supplied to the Iraq Petroleum Co in April 1948 had an NR6/PI engine. Economics stopped further progress at that stage, yet ironically, 20 years or so later, petrol injection was taken up for high-performance cars, Thornycroft's pioneer venture being largely forgotten.

South African Railways, seemingly a 'natural' customer for the PI engine, opted to continue with conventional petrol engines, including a carburettor version of the NR6 called the NR6/AP, giving 123bhp at 2,300rpm, this type being fitted in 39 Trusty VF models in 1948-9. The other petrol engine chosen by SAR was a revival of the 11.3-litre 4³/₄in bore and 6¹/₂in stroke engine size whose roots went back to the Hathi tractor of 1924. This time it was known as the GRN6, of conventional overhead-valve design, though

Below:
South African Railways continued its independent line of thought on vehicle design. The SA model was nominally a Trusty variant, though its specification pointed the way to later Big Ben models as well as inheriting characteristics of earlier SAR versions of the XB and XF types. The engine was the GRN6/1 petrol engine of 11.3-litre capacity and the chassis retained the cross-country capability given by the Thornycroft rear bogie, as demonstrated here. It was built in two versions, the vehicle shown being on chassis 49592, delivered in May 1948, the first of the 86 with 7-ton load rating designed to suit the three-compartment body carrying two classes of passengers and goods, in this case built by Metro-Cammell. *IAL*

noteworthy in having two Solex carburettors – the output was 155bhp at 2,000rpm. A special heavy-duty forward-control six-wheeler was designated SA/GRN6 and was designed to run at up to 19 tons gross and haul a 12-ton trailer. At first, it was designated as a Trusty, and an example from the first orders for 96 was shown at the 1948 Earl's Court Show. A subsequent development put the weights up to 20 tons and 25 tons respectively, and the engine became the GRN6/1 with 160bhp; some 186 of these SA types were produced, creating the basis from which the later Big Ben range was developed – some had bus bodywork. In 1948-9 there were also 60 of a South African Railways version of the VF, the SAVF, again with the GRN6/1 engine.

During the war years plans had been made to re-enter the mainstream bus market in Britain, once peace returned. Enquiries on design preferences had been made to several major bus operators during the sales department's study early in 1943, with enough encouraging reaction to be pursued further. In August 1945, the Government, at that date still controlling all vehicle production, issued a list of makes of vehicle which would be available in 1946, and Thornycroft was duly included among those to offer 'double and single deck (heavy PSV) chassis'. Publication in such a list implied approval for such production and assurance of material availability, notably steel.

Two models were planned – the DG/NR6 and SG/NR6, for double- and single-deck bodywork respectively – in most respects conforming to conventional practice of the day, with chassis broadly similar to the 1939-40 prototype but with the NR6 engine as standard. Here again, there had been calls for Gardner engines in the wartime consultation exercise. The radiator was quite similar to the postwar

Thornycroft's plan to re-enter the mainstream bus market after the war started with considerable promise, the first of a pair of DG/NR6 chassis, number 48064, intended for double-deck bodywork being built in about 1946. At first, its transmission incorporated a fluid flywheel and what was basically a conventional gearbox arranged to operate in a preselective fashion. Attempts to make it work satisfactorily failed, that particular chassis eventually being bodied in July 1952 by Thurgood as a 35-seat single-deck bus for use by the Thornycroft shipyard at Woolston, as shown here.
Thornycroft Society

Below left:
Only one customer received a batch of the postwar SG/NR6 model, this being the Bristol Co-operative Society, an existing Thornycroft customer for goods models, which ran a coach fleet using the fleetname 'Queen of the Road'. A batch of five was supplied in the spring of 1948, these having bodywork by Longwell Green, a Bristol concern, though the style had a strong resemblance to the contemporary standard Duple design. As operated, they are understood to have had conventional gearboxes, possibly from new.
Thornycroft Society

Below:
The final chapter in the SG story was the production of a pair of 8ft-wide 18ft 6in bonneted chassis with left-hand drive, type SG8/NR6, perhaps with recollections of earlier success with Egyptian General in mind. This one, 51718, was bodied in September 1948 by Thurgood to a design incorporating an insulated roof. It appeared in the demonstration park at the Commercial Motor Show that year and was sent out to Kuwait, but returned and was latterly used in the works transport fleet.
Thornycroft Society

Trusty style though with the top not quite so rounded and having a squared-up nearside front wing assembly, enabling a pair of flush-fitting headlamps to be used.

A new combination of fluid flywheel and what was called a synchromesh self-shifting gearbox, intended to be standard for the bus models, proved unsatisfactory and delayed progress. In the event, the whole bus project never got beyond the prototype stage and no buses reached the municipal or major company sectors, despite sales successes in comparable circumstances by firms such as Crossley, Foden and Maudslay in that period. Interest in the project within the firm seemed to wane, and Sydney Dack's departure may have been a factor.

In the event, two DG/NR6 prototype chassis (48064/5) were built, the first eventually being bodied in July 1952 as a single-deck bus for Thornycroft's Woolston shipyard. The only 'outside' order was for five SG/NR6 (49682-6) models, bodied by Longwell Green as coaches for the Bristol Co-operative Society and delivered in the spring of 1948. There were also two normal-control SG8/NR6 chassis (51717/8), the first being bodied by Thurgood in September 1948 and displayed in the demonstration park at the 1948 Earl's Court Show.

Below:
A user of the Nippy HF/ER4 model in passenger form was David MacBrayne Ltd, with six in 1947 having Harkness bodywork seating between seven and 20 passengers and, in 1949, a further six with Croft 20-seat bodywork. The last of the latter, based on chassis 52490 and registered HGG 359, is seen when in the service of McLachlan of Tayvallich, following its withdrawal from service by MacBrayne in 1962. It is one of two of these vehicles which survive. *Thornycroft Society*

Right:
The normal-control version of the Trident first seen at the 1948 Show was given a front end in the newly fashionable style with the radiator concealed behind an ornamental grille. *IAL*

Below right:
The Trident in forward-control form retained the general appearance of the smaller models in the range, though the styling of the cab was mildly updated for 1950 production, as shown here. The view also shows the slightly cranked frame characteristic of mid-range Thornycroft models of that period. *IAL*

The postwar Nippy was sold for passenger use in very small numbers – Tillingbourne Valley took another forward-control Nippy in 1946, this time an HF/ER4 but again with Thurgood 20-seat body. David MacBrayne Ltd took six of the same model in 1947 for its services in the Scottish highlands and islands, bodied by Harkness, in some cases as combined passenger and goods models, and a further six, bodied by Croft, in 1949.

The postwar Labour Government's policy of nationalisation was causing concern, and in April 1948 action was taken to split the vehicle manufacturing section of the company at Basingstoke, perceived as threatened in this way, together with the closely associated Reading engine works, into a separate subsidiary, given the title Transport Equipment (Thornycroft) Ltd, while John I. Thornycroft Ltd continued with ship and boat building at Woolston and Hampton as well as acting as parent company to TE(T) Ltd, including some publicity and sales services. Shipbuilding again turned to civilian work, two passenger ships built in 1947-8 being supplied to French and Egyptian operators for services across the Mediterranean.

Left:
The same front-end style was scaled up, with the headlamps more widely spaced, for the bonneted versions of the Trusty range. Seen examining an ON six-wheeler in June 1950 are G. MacKenzie-Junner, editor of *The Commercial Motor* (in the dark suit), Roger Thornycroft and, nearest the camera, R. F. Newman, the latter two being respectively Sales Director and Managing Director of the Basingstoke works. *IAL*

Below left:
Argentina continued to be an important market. This Trusty ON/NR6 with locally built cab and all-metal tipping body was supplied to the State Gas Department, Buenos Aires, through the Thornycroft branch in that city. *IAL*

At Basingstoke, the Trident RG was introduced as a new lighter 7^1/$_2$-ton at the 1948 Show, the emphasis being initially on the bonneted RGN export version, although regular production did not begin until 1950; there were also RH and RHN versions. It had a new 5.51-litre diesel engine, the CR6, with 3^7/$_8$in by 4^3/$_4$in bore and stroke. This had direct injection and developed 78bhp at 1,900rpm, but the RGN is probably best remembered for the new style of front end, with radiator concealed behind a full-width pressed-steel cowl having a horizontally slatted grille.

The Sturdy Star was a mildly updated version of the Sturdy, the ZG, using a new direct-injection version of the 4.1-litre engine called the TR6/DI, though this latter was also introduced on later ZE and YE models. There was also a bonneted version, type ZGN. A four-cylinder equivalent of the TR6 was the TR4, bringing the swept volume down to 2.7 litres and in one form giving only 41bhp, but this was used by British Railways in some Nippy models on delivery work, giving 19mpg.

The new front-end design for the export Trident was scaled up slightly for use on overseas bonneted Trusty models which appeared in postwar form with the NR6/MV engine in 1949. They comprised the VN two-axle model, available initially as a tractor for use with semi-trailers, but also later as a load carrier, though built only in modest numbers, and the ON six-wheeler, of which production runs of 25 and then 50 were built in 1949-52.

The Mighty Antar

However, the big new development of 1949, in all senses, was the Mighty Antar, designed initially to meet a specification from the Iraq Petroleum Co for a vehicle capable of hauling sections of pipe in 60-ton loads for a 560-mile-long oil pipeline to be constructed from Kirkuk to the port of Baniyas in the Mediterranean, still in use today. This involved running over a desert track for 250 miles. The result was advertised as 'Britain's biggest tractor', designed to operate at gross train weights of up to 100 tons with a

Below:
The first Mighty Antar, seen on trial with a semi-trailer loaded with test weights, before final painting and delivery to the Iraq Petroleum Co Ltd in March 1950. Two radiators were mounted side by side, each connected to one bank of the Rover Meteorite V8 diesel engine of 18-litre capacity. The 11ft 6in width made it necessary to seek special permission for movements in Britain on public roads. *IAL*

semi-trailer made by Cranes (Dereham) Ltd, although also suitable to run in solo form at 32 tons gross.

It was a bonneted six-wheeler, 31ft 10in long and some 11ft 6in wide, weighing 15½ tons unladen with cab and on 14.00-24 tyres. The engine was a Rover Meteorite indirect-injection diesel, an 18-litre V8 unit derived from the Rolls-Royce Merlin V12 aero engine of Battle of Britain fame, developing 250bhp at 2,000rpm, a seemingly modest figure by the standards of half a century later, yet the Antar was the most powerful road vehicle in the country at the time. There was a conventional four-speed constant-mesh gearbox with a three-speed auxiliary gearbox, both of Thornycroft make as usual on the company's products. The rear bogie, made by Kirkstall, with worm and epicyclic reduction gearing, had suspension of traditional Thornycroft style. Clayton Dewandre supplied the air-pressure system for the brakes and assisting the handbrake and clutch action – there was hydraulic power-assistance for the steering. The frame was made from ³/₈in plate and the general proportions were nearer to railway than motor vehicle standards.

The characteristic appearance, with the radiator grille almost the full width of the vehicle, was due to the use of two radiators mounted side by side, each connected to one

Above:
Part of the route over which the first fleet of Mighty Antar vehicles operated with 60-ton loads of pipes involved crossing a desert on which dust storms could be a problem, as seen here, but reliability proved to be good. *IAL*

bank of cylinders in the vee-form engine, designed to cope with ambient temperatures of up to 120°F. The 'T' emblem formed the middle of the word 'Antar' on the grille. There were 35 Antars in the original IPC contract, numbered 53781-815, the first ready for testing at the end of 1949 and delivery in March 1950, with the rest of the fleet following by May 1951. Charles E. Burton, the Chief Designer, had the privilege of telling the story to a meeting of the Institution of Mechanical Engineers in September 1951, by which time the vehicles had covered over half a million miles without any disabling breakdown.

This success led to the opening up of other applications for the Antar as well as bringing valuable prestige and publicity to the company. The model was too large for general use on public roads in Britain, being restricted to pre-arranged routes even for testing purposes, so at first it was a rare sight, but it caught the public imagination.

10. A Move towards Specialisation

Renewed international tension and the war in Korea, in which British forces were involved under the United Nations, led to fresh orders for military vehicles in the early 1950s. The idea of moving tanks on suitably designed transporters had grown in favour, and the Antar (officially the Mighty Antar, though colloquially the adjective was usually dropped; later there was to be a specific model lacking it) opened up new possibilities in this direction. The Army was using the Rover Meteor engine, based on the Rolls-Royce Merlin aero engine, for tank propulsion, these engines retaining the original 27-litre swept volume, 12-cylinder vee layout and petrol as fuel, though derated to give 600-700bhp.

The idea of using the closely related Rover Meteorite 18-litre V8 engine in petrol form for tank transporter duty had obvious appeal, giving many common features with the tank engine and a little more power than the diesel version, with 285bhp. This became standard for the first generations of Mighty Antar for the British

Above:
This long-wheelbase Mighty Antar, one of three dating from late 1951, was used by Shell in North Borneo and had a self-loading capability, the mobile drilling unit for an oil-well, mounted on a skid, being hauled by winch on to the special body, during which process the front of the vehicle lifted completely from the ground. The total load thus carried was 28 tons. *IAL*

The early military version of the Mighty Antar became a familiar sight in Britain, although these four, seen heading north through Banbury on trade plates and having lifting rings on the front and rearmost wheels, were evidently heading for the docks, presumably Liverpool, and thence bound overseas. *IAL*

Left:
It seems that the owner of this 1951 Sturdy Star believed in getting full value from its 5-ton load rating. *IAL*

Below:
Thornycroft supplied six buses on RHN/CR6 chassis to George Wimpey & Co for use in the Lebanon in 1951 – bodywork was by Park Royal. *IAL*

Bottom left:
The days of the Raj may have been over but Englishmen going out in the midday sun could still be seen suitably attired in Poona in 1952, where the Municipal Transport system used Thornycroft buses, in this case a Sturdy, with 24-seat body by General Motors, Bombay. *IAL*

Army, soon to become quite familiar on British roads, as they went into large-scale service. They had quite a distinctive sound – the engines spent much of the time at fairly high revs – not unduly noisy in relation to the weights being moved.

However, the uneven tickover was a disappointment to anyone familiar with V8 car engines – for production reasons, the vee-angle was the same 60° as on the original V12 design instead of being the correct 90° for a V8.

Early military versions of the Antar were ballasted to draw separate trailers but later ones were linked to semi-trailers. The wheelbase was reduced to 15ft 6in, also adopted for some civilian versions which followed, though they usually had diesel engines. A one-off oddity built in 1952

Above:
Dorman, Long & Co Ltd was a regular Thornycroft customer. This Nippy HF/ER4 model dated from early 1951, by which date the style of cab used, almost unaltered since 1943 and which had then seemed agreeably modern, was looking rather dated. *IAL*

was a two-axle version intended for use with earth-moving equipment, the rear axle being directly attached to the chassis and the vehicle relying on the cushioning effect of the very large rear tyres.

More successful were a pair of Antar six-wheel tractors (54780/1) built in 1953 for use with a drawbar trailer to carry machinery weighing up to 120 tons for the Snowy Mountain Hydro-Electric Authority in New South Wales, Australia, but tried out before shipment by transporting a turbo-generator from the AEI works in Birmingham to Newport.

The Shell concern used a self-loading long-wheelbase version in North Borneo. However, the main demand was military, and by the mid-1950s the Antar had been put into the traditional Thornycroft system with production batches of 100, 50 and most of what was probably planned as

another 50 completed in the 1953-7 period, with deliveries to the armies of the Netherlands, India, Burma and Iraq, although the British Army was the main user, graduating to what was called the Mark II, used with a semi-trailer.

Another aspect of military need was for a new generation of heavy-duty 6x4 forward-control goods model for more general duties, and here the work done for South African Railways provided the basis for what evolved into an important new range – the Big Ben. Like the South African SAR model, the SM, of which 617 were supplied to the British Army in 1952-5, used the GRN6/2 petrol engine, developing up to 170bhp, the appearance being quite similar to the forward-control Trusty, though subtly heavier-looking.

The market for the small-to-medium end of the range was becoming more competitive. However, for a time the Trident, with RH 6-ton and RG 8-ton models, both having the CR6 5.51-litre diesel, sold quite strongly when it went into production in 1950, even though up against the Leyland Comet and, slightly later, the AEC Mercury. The Sturdy Star ZG 5-tonner, with the TR6/DI 4.14-litre engine giving 61bhp at 2,000rpm or the ER4 petrol engine, also appeared that year. Normal-control RHN, RHN and ZGN options of the foregoing types were built in smaller numbers for export. In 1951 the Nippy Star HG also appeared with TR6/DI or ER4 option, thus bringing the diesel option into the smallest models offered. For the time being, this helped to hold off the challenge of Ford and Bedford in the range up to about 6 tons. The 'plain' Nippy continued for a while for

Left:
The new Motor Panels cab gave quite a stylish look. It was applied to the Trident from 1952, these two RG 8-ton models in the Fisons fleet dating from 1955 – they are seen at the firm's Barking works. *IAL*

Left:
The Nippy Star had also received the new cab by 1954, when this HG with TR6/DI engine was supplied to Timothy Whites & Taylors, owner of a nationwide chain of chemists and household goods stores. Its Thornycroft vans were then a familiar sight in every high street. *ATC*

Below:
Representative of later Trusty PF eight-wheelers with the NR6/MV engine is this example, one of a pair (59550/1) supplied complete with all-metal cab and platform body to the Angus Milling Co Ltd of Kirriemuir in November 1953. *IAL*

Right:
This Trusty RF six-wheeler, 59858, was supplied to Morey's (Verwood) Ltd, of Ringwood, Hants, as a 10cu yd dump truck, with half cab. The Newton Chambers NCK excavator seen in the picture also had a Thornycroft NR6 engine similar to that in the Trusty. *IAL*

Below right:
The Nubian TF model, originally designed to meet a wartime Army requirement for a 4x4 vehicle, took on a fresh lease of life in the 1950s as an airfield crash tender. These three for the Belgian Congo had bodywork by Sun Engineering (Richmond) Ltd and equipment by Walter Kidde. The high build of the TF chassis remains evident in its new clothes. *IAL*

Above:
The Big Ben was beginning to develop into a remarkably complex range of models. The forward-control types were apt to look like slightly overgrown Trusty models, although the appearance of this one was slightly disguised by the stoneguard fitted to the radiator. It had a soil-testing laboratory body built by Normand and is believed to be one of two SMC/KRN6 models, chassis 59954/5, supplied to John Mowlem & Co Ltd in the winter of 1956-7. *IAL*

Below:
The bonneted Big Ben types had a grille of similar style to the earlier Antar models but reduced in size to suit the single radiator behind it. What by then was being called the standard steel cab suited the model remarkably well, even though the protective shield disguised its appearance somewhat. This 6x4 example with 15cu yd dump-truck body was evidently an SLCN model of the mid-1950s. *IAL*

specialist users, notably in bonneted left-hand GF form for the Lewin road sweeper – it was produced, latterly often with the four-cylinder TR4/DI diesel engine but still sometimes the ER4 petrol unit, until the late 1950s, its mid-1930s origins still very evident.

The forward-control cab designs of these models were becoming rather dated, but the Sturdy Star and Trident got a major boost in terms of appearance in the spring of 1952 when a new Motor Panels pressed-steel cab was introduced – the Nippy Star followed a little later. It was in the much more rounded style by then in favour on cars, with deeper and more strongly raked vee windscreen glasses. It was also taken up by Guy for its comparable models, but the distinctive Thornycroft grille with 'T' emblem left no room for doubt as to the make of chassis even when viewed from a distance. For a time, Thornycroft continued to attract a reasonable level of orders for these lighter models. For example, a production series of 500 Nippy Star and Nippy models had begun in 1951 but had not quite been filled in when the last vehicles within it were completed in 1958,

Top right:
The Big Ben was very largely an export model, among the few civilian users in Britain being the National Coal Board. This SMC with KRN6 oil engine is thought to be chassis 58037, delivered to the NCB's Yorkshire Area for use in open-cast mining in 1956 – two similar vehicles were supplied in 1957. *IAL*

Right:
The KRN6 oil engine of 11.3-litre swept volume announced in 1952 was larger in external dimensions than other makers' engines of similar capacity 'stretched' from smaller units but was designed for heavy-duty applications. This example has a gearbox with remote change-speed for installation in a forward-control Big Ben. *IAL*

though the picture was complicated by special order batches outside it and the introduction of a successor model.

The Trusty range continued to sell in modest numbers but was handicapped as a result of the vehicle policy adopted by British Road Services, the nationalised haulage concern formed in 1948 taking over most long-distance goods operation. It standardised largely on Leyland and AEC eight-wheelers, although a few PF models were supplied. The last production PF eight-wheeler was delivered in 1956, bringing the total built to 248, or about one per fortnight since its introduction.

Where Thornycroft scored was in its ability to produce more specialised types of vehicle and to tailor them to meet individual customers' needs in ways competitors geared to larger-scale production could not match. Some existing models found new applications, an example being the Nubian TF 4x4 model, by then available with the CR6 5.51-litre diesel engine, although the AC4/1 5.17-litre four-cylinder petrol engine, basically a 1934 design, was still offered. The type, running at up to $10\frac{1}{2}$ tons gross, had found a new application as an airfield crash tender, nimble enough to reach a crashed aircraft without delay either on the tarmac or, if need be, on soft uneven ground.

For such applications in particular, an important Nubian option added in 1953 was the Rolls-Royce B80 petrol engine having eight cylinders arranged in-line and of 5.67-litre capacity. This was of the same design as the 4.25-litre six-cylinder engines used in the earlier postwar Rolls-Royce and Bentley cars – the overhead-inlet side-exhaust layout revived a principle favoured on Thornycroft engines of the early 1920s. The B80 gave 140bhp at 3,750rpm in this application, putting the performance into a quite different league from the 86bhp offered by the AC4/1.

An important development was the introduction of the KRN6 diesel engine, announced in time for the 1952 Show, which in effect turned the Big Ben from purely a military or 'South African' model into a range offered for more general

sale, although catering for a specialised market, often for off-road use. This engine was the latest in the long line of Thornycroft 11.3-litre six-cylinder engines with $4^{3}/_{4}$in bore and $6^{1}/_{2}$in stroke, developing 155bhp at 1,900rpm. The Big Ben types listed in 1953 were the SAR – as might be guessed, for South African Railways – and the SMC, each available with the GRN6/2 petrol engine or the KRN6 diesel. Among the few users in Britain was the National Coal Board, choosing the type for operation on open-cast mining sites.

Technological development did not stand still and Thornycroft was among the pioneer users of turbocharging to increase engine output. The KRN6 engine had been designed with this in mind from the beginning and the KRN6/S so equipped, pushing its power to 200bhp, was announced in 1954. A leading light in this development was Ken Martlew, then Experimental Engineer. Another quite different line of development in that period, well in advance of its more widespread adoption on commercial vehicles, was in the use of glassfibre-reinforced plastics, mainly for cab structures. Among the first applications was for a Sturdy Star demonstrator with cab of similar outline to the Motor Panels design but with slender windscreen frame.

The Nubian range was extended in 1954 by the introduction of the TFA 6x6 model, initially with the choice of CR6 diesel or Rolls-Royce B80 petrol engine, extending the gross weight to a nominal 14 tons. It used the classic Thornycroft rear bogie, in much the same basic design as on

the A3 model back in the late 1920s. The chassis design was revised in many details and production TFA models had a noticeably lower driving position than the TF. This found two quite distinct markets: the diesel version was favoured largely by oil companies as a cross-country model while the petrol version was chosen as an airfield crash tender for both civilian and military applications – it soon became a familiar sight at airports in most parts of the world. A further Nubian development was the introduction in 1956 of the TFB 4x4 version which brought the later design features to the four-wheel model, superseding the TF. Very often this too had the B80, although the CR6/1 was offered. Nubians were built in production runs, usually of 100, repeating every couple of years or so, forming an important part of the works output in this period.

The Rolls-Royce B81 engine, of similar design to the B80 but of 6.52-litre capacity, tended to be more often specified for the TFA from the later 1950s. These straight-eight B80 and B81 engines were never offered for general sale in cars, the only 17 examples of the Rolls-Royce Phantom IV sold being supplied only to Royalty or other Heads of State, yet the refined sound of the engines was familiar in the Thornycroft works yard in the late 1950s and 1960s when what were eventually several hundred Nubian models were so powered.

In the mid-1950s, new generations of several models began to appear and, as in earlier times, new engines formed the basis of new model ranges, although the economics of making engines in modest quantities was becoming increasingly difficult and, indeed the QR6, of 9.83-litre swept volume, and the JR6, of 4.18 litres, both announced in 1955, were to prove the last major new designs to appear from Thornycroft. The JR6 retained the cylinder dimensions of the TR6/DI which it superseded, but was extensively redesigned in an effort to reduce manufacturing costs – it developed 80bhp at 2,600rpm initially, later increased to 85bhp at the same speed.

The QR6 at last provided Thornycroft with an answer to the AEC 590 and Leyland O.600 engines of similar size. It was a conventional six-cylinder direct-injection engine of up-to-date design, having the $4^{3}/_{4}$in bore size shared with the KRN6 but with a shorter stroke of the odd-seeming size of

5.65in to give a 9.83-litre swept volume and indeed a very different, more compact and lighter engine – the output was 130bhp at 2,000rpm. It was quite a refined unit, and basically sound, though there were some teething troubles with cracking of cylinder heads, the type of trouble apt to occur when resources for in-service testing are limited, adding to the problems of breaking into a market against established designs of good reputation. The new Trusty PK/QR6 eight-wheeler first appeared at the 1955 Scottish Show, although production did not begin until mid-1957, when one was offered to the technical press for test. Understandably, the phrase 'the ideal eight-wheeler' applied to it by John F. Moon of *The Commercial Motor* was adopted as a sales slogan. From the driver's viewpoint, power-assisted steering was the most outstanding new feature, then still regarded as a luxury on production vehicles of any kind, although Thornycroft had gained early experience with the Mighty Antar. Overall, the PK was perhaps the most 'civilised' eight-wheeler of its generation. The standard cab was based on the Motor Panels design used on smaller models, though wider and having a rather angular, horizontally slatted grille not unlike that used on bonneted Trident and Trusty models.

Below:
The Trusty PK/QR6 went into production in 1957, one of the first to enter service being 61311, supplied to T. J. E. Price (Cardiff) Ltd in July of that year. Here the steel cab took on a further different look when mounted on the square-cut cab base of this model, with a grille design rather similar to that of the bonneted Trusty. It was an impressive design but relatively expensive, and sales were slow, only six reaching operators that year. *Thornycroft Society*

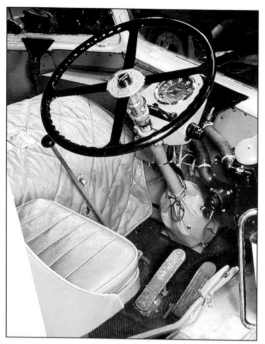

At the other end of the scale in the home market range were the new models powered by the JR6, called Swift and Swiftsure, which also appeared in 1957. The Swift was designated GL and designed to run at up to 7 tons gross, which implied a nominal payload of 4^1/$_2$ tons. The Swiftsure HL and PL were in the 5^1/$_2$-6-ton class. At first they retained the Motor Panels cab in original form, and thus looked very like the Nippy Star or Sturdy Star models they replaced.

For a time around 1957-8, overall Basingstoke works output dropped to about one chassis per day, though, fortuitously, a contract to recondition existing military Antar models which had deteriorated, mainly due to lack of use, helped to keep the workshops busy.

Sales were becoming increasingly difficult, especially on the intensely competitive home market, and a reason for delaying putting new models into production was sometimes a desire to gain time to sell existing models for which parts were still in stock.

The initial stock works order for the PK eight-wheeler was issued in December, 1955 just after the first example had been exhibited, but it was not until March 1957, just as PK production eventually got under way, that one was issued for the other new two- and three-axle Trusty models with the QR6 engine, to supersede the NR6-powered versions. The resulting VK and RK were not publicly announced until the 1958 Show, although some types had then begun production.

11. An Action-filled Finale

From an engineering viewpoint, the last few years of Thornycroft's independent existence as a vehicle maker were full of activity, mainly concentrated on the heavier models. The firm still had a strong position in its role as a specialist manufacturer, with first-class engineering expertise yet small enough to be largely free from bureaucracy, allowing great flexibility. The vehicles built were not very great in number, but they were mostly large, well equipped and often designed to suit specific needs, the kind of work in which the Basingstoke factory excelled.

The new normal-control Big Ben models were in production from 1957. Thereafter, the majority of Big Ben output was of this layout, the main types being the SLCN 6x4 type and the equivalent SLDN 6x6 version, while the SLEN was built as 6x4 but with provision for easy conversion to 6x6 in service. Generally they were rated at about 31 tons gross as solo vehicles or 60 tons gross train weight in articulated form, but there was also an SMCN tractor version to run at up to 45 tons GTW. The KRN6 engine was nominally standard but the 200bhp KRN6/S was often specified, notably for tractor units. Even in standard form, these were quite massive-looking machines.

In addition, the British Army required a further supply of Mighty Antar tank transporters and by late 1957 work on the first of a new type was in hand. There had been a fresh review of possible engine types and in 1957 one chassis (61182) received an AEC AV1100 engine, an 18-litre in-line six-cylinder unit intended mainly for a large dump-truck, requiring an extended bonnet.

By then, Rolls-Royce had introduced its own range of diesel engines. The power unit chosen for what became generally known as the Antar Mark III was the C8SFL, again an eight-cylinder engine but this time of in-line layout. It is noteworthy that the Army preferred this to a turbocharged version of the basically similar six-cylinder version of this engine design soon to be chosen by other Antar customers. The C8SFL was of slightly smaller, 16.2-

Above:
Most orders for Big Ben models from 1957 were of the bonneted type, early examples including three SLDN/KRN6/S for the Qatar Petroleum Co Ltd, 59958-60, delivered in May of that year. One is seen being loaded with a Woodfield Ideco portable drilling rig before moving off a well. *IAL*

litre swept volume than the Meteorite V8 unit but produced more power, at 333bhp, than the earlier models, either petrol or diesel. Inevitably a straight-eight was also substantially longer than a vee-form engine, and here too the chassis had to be redesigned to accept it, with a longer though narrower bonnet, the grille being similar to that on Big Ben bonneted models – the cab was yet another version of the standard steel design. New box-shaped front wings accommodated large oil-bath air cleaners. An initial batch of three Antar Mark IIIs (61183-5) were delivered in February-March 1958 with two more (61187/8) in March 1959. There was a pause while assessment took place, but noteworthy among later batches was a War Office order for 175 delivered in 1962-4.

Meanwhile, there were further Antar III variants, such as two (61189/90) with the C6T turbocharged six-cylinder version of the Rolls-Royce engine built for Associated Electrical Industries in April 1960 for shipment to Argentina for use on a power station contract. The Kuwait Government also took the C6T engine in five examples later that year. However, Pakistan chose the eight-cylinder engine for a batch in 1960-1.

Left:
Odd man out among Antars was this one, chassis 61182 dating from 1957, fitted with an AEC AV1100 engine, housed under an extended bonnet with Big Ben-type radiator grille but with the early style of cab. It was used in comparative tests but the decision went to the Rolls-Royce C8SFL engine. *Thornycroft Society*

Left:

An increasingly familiar sight whenever the Army was moving tanks, from the 1960s until a few years ago, was the Antar Mark III with the Rolls-Royce C8SFL engine. One of the production vehicles of 1962-3 operating with semi-trailer is seen here. *Thornycroft Society*

Below left:
Externally similar to the military Antar III was a pair of left-hand-drive tractors (61189/90) with Rolls-Royce C6T turbocharged engines supplied to Associated Electrical Industries Ltd in 1960 for use on a power station contract in Buenos Aires, Argentina. They were designed to haul independent trailers carrying transformers weighing up to 97 tons and thus had ballast bodies – a 50,000lb winch was mounted behind the cab. *IAL*

At this time, the demand for specialised oilfield vehicles was rising. Examples of the bonneted Big Ben models were soon being built for service in Argentina and South Africa, but the Middle East remained the centre of interest; a report made by A. K. Southon to the Thornycroft management in July 1961 outlined events in Libya. Two SLDN/KRN6 tankers and trailers had been supplied to Gordon Woodroffe, a transport specialist, delivering oil to drilling rigs accessible over fairly firm ground, reported as giving sterling service. American oil companies in the area were mainly running Kenworth 6x6 vehicles with Cummins 300bhp engines on very large 18.00-25 sand tyres in desert conditions but were keen to spend sterling balances on British equipment.

After a meeting in May 1958, there was a degree of decisiveness rare in Thornycroft's history as a vehicle maker. Two prototypes of a model called the Big Ben Sandmaster were to be built, using the same 18.00-25 size of sand tyres – significantly, Scammell, the strongest British competitor, decided it could not put its equivalent model, the Super Constructor, onto such tyres. Moreover, it was also decided that the Antar be similarly developed, using even larger 21.00-25 tyres.

These amounted to new models, for the bigger tyres required wider-spaced bogie axles, itself requiring further design work by Kirkstall, as well as the more obvious changes. The first of the Big Ben version, for use by Gulf, entered service in February 1959, tests showing that it could outperform the Kenworth despite having less power. Another was sold to Boccanera and an order from BP followed, for seven of the same type.

In mid-1959, Esso put out a specification for a larger vehicle on sand tyres to some 75 makers, leading to a short list of three, Kenworth, Rotinoff and Thornycroft, the outcome being the choice of the Antar Sandmaster with Rolls-Royce C6 turbocharged engine and Self-Changing

Below:
The Big Ben in Sandmaster form looked fully as massive as an Antar, as demonstrated in this photograph, believed to show the original vehicle delivered to the Gulf Oil Company in Libya in February 1959 which proved capable of outperforming an American Kenworth 853 model of comparable specification. *IAL*

Gears semi-automatic transmission – this latter proved to stand up to the operating conditions better than a conventional clutch and gearbox. It used a fluid coupling and RV30 epicyclic gearbox, operated by a control giving sequential changes, rather like a modern racing or rally car, and became an option for other models. Twelve Antar Sandmasters were built for use by Esso in Libya, the first being ready in September 1960. The oilfield equipment they hauled on massive semi-trailers gave a gross train weight of over 100 tons, moved quite easily over a soft sand surface.

Meanwhile, another variant of design married the heavy-duty Antar frame, rear bogie and front axle, in this case on conventional 14.00-24 tyres and in long-wheelbase form, with the KRN6 engine and gearbox assembly as used in a Big Ben. This had been introduced in response to a specification by the Oil Companies Materials Committee and was announced at the 1958 Earl's Court show, officially called the Antar, without the Mighty prefix; the model designation was MA/KRN6/S. The result, given the number 61186, looked very like a Big Ben, distinguishable mainly by the heavier-duty wheels – it was designed to run in solo form at 46$\frac{1}{2}$ tons gross. Later the KRN6-series engines were revised in design, becoming the K6 or K6/S.

Renewed interest was also being placed in bonneted versions of the Trusty. The first of the new RKN six-wheeler chassis, using the QR6 engine, were built towards the end of 1958, seven being for Basrah Petroleum and two right-hand examples for Australia; left-hand steering was far more common, as also applied to the larger oilfield types. Early RKN models retained the 'streamlined' front end of the previous equivalent ON/NR6 version.

Here too, major design variations arose. Another American customer for vehicles for use in Libya was the Halliburton Oilwell Cementation Co, which standardised on Cummins engines, the latter concern then producing a range of heavy-duty in-line six-cylinder engines, among which even the 11-litre NH180 unit of 180bhp chosen for a Trusty RKN tractive unit was too big to fit into the then standard bonneted Trusty front-end. It was decided to abandon the ON-style sheet metalwork, adopting a simpler style, with the same radiator grille as used on the bonneted Big Ben, though with mudguards having a squared-off front face. This vehicle was numbered 62074 in a series of varied Trusty types and delivered in October 1959 for use with a Dyson semi-trailer.

A requirement for sand tyres also existed for the Trusty RKN/QR6, in this case the Atlas 16.00-20, chosen for 10 to be supplied via Woodroffe for use in Libya by Esso. There was again a substantial redesign, with an extended bogie, though the new front end with Big Ben grille just introduced to accommodate the Cummins engine lent itself to the enlarged mudguards needed fairly simply. These, and a long-wheelbase RKN/QR6 also on sand tyres for Halliburton, were built with standard gearboxes, but a further batch for Esso had the RV30. Thereafter it was decided to use the new-style front end for all RKN and VKN types; orders for the latter were yet to follow.

Halliburton specified the Cummins NRT6B turbocharged six-cylinder 12.18-litre in-line engine developing 305bhp for a batch of five SLDN models (62483-7) delivered in April-

July 1960. In this case Allison Torquematic automatic transmission was specified. Mr Southon's 1961 report noted that, in all, there were 56 Thornycroft vehicles then operating in Libya, comprising the 12 Antar Sandmasters, 16 Big Bens, 21 Trustys and seven Nubians, these latter including two each of the TFA and TFB types in use at Tripoli airport.

Meanwhile, there had been developments in home-market models. The NS6 7.88-litre engine had been introduced in 1956 as a final development from the NR6, improvements in breathing increasing net power output to 109bhp at 1,800rpm. It was offered from that year in a rare Trusty variant, the VL – a production batch of six were numbered 61158-63 and delivered to various users between 1957 and 1959, but in effect the type was a stepping-stone to a new medium-range model. This was the Mastiff ML, also with the NS6 engine, introduced in time for the 1958 Show, in response to the revised regulations permitting 14 tons gross on a two-axle vehicle. It could also be counted as Thornycroft's answer to models such as the AEC Mercury. As introduced, it had the same style of cab as the early PK, VK, etc but the front axle was set back slightly. Again, it drew strong approval from John Moon of *The Commercial Motor*, who obtained 14.4mpg on a fully laden run, with special praise for the

Left:
When an American concern, Halliburton, specified the Cummins NH180 engine for a Trusty RKN tractor, it proved impossible to accommodate it in the front end inherited from the ON model, and the solution used a slightly longer conventional bonnet, together with the Big Ben grille – subsequently this was adopted as standard for the RKN and VKN models. In this view, the Halliburton RKN/NH180, chassis 62074, is seen coupled to its Dyson semi-trailer before shipment in 1959. *ATC*

Below left:
The use of large-section sand tyres was extended to Trusty RKN models to be used for oilfield work in areas with soft sand in Libya. The Esso concern took 10 examples, 62083-92, on the 14ft 6in-wheelbase version of the model with standard QR6 engines, the new-style front end proving quite readily adaptable to the large tyres with suitably modified mudguards. One is seen in service, carrying a Failing drilling rig for exploration duties. *IAL*

Bottom:
The Trusty VL was a short-lived variant using the NS6 engine, the latter updated from the NR6. Holloway Bros (London) Ltd took delivery of two in July 1958. Both are visible in this view, with the same firm's 1954 Trusty PF/NR6 eight-wheeler between them. All three had sliding cab doors, a feature sometimes favoured on London-based vehicles to minimise the problem of opening them in busy streets.
Thornycroft Society

Top right:
The Mastiff ML/NS6 introduced to take full advantage of the 14-ton gross rating in 1958 reverted to the concept of a slightly increased front overhang, rather in the manner of the original Trusty PE of prewar days, though with styling otherwise rather like the PK in original form. An early ML demonstrator is seen here. *Thornycroft Society*

Right:
There had been a number of glass-fibre cab designs retaining the basic outline of the standard steel cab, sometimes with minor alterations, but a completely fresh design with wrap-round windscreen was introduced, at first for the smaller models, at the 1958 Show. This long-wheelbase Swiftsure was placed in service by Simmonds Aerocessories Ltd in 1959. *IAL*

quiet and smooth running – the test vehicle had an optional six-speed gearbox. A production run of 100 found buyers between 1958 and 1961, often existing Thornycroft users. The QR6 engine was offered as an option from 1960 but the NS6 version continued to be popular.

A stylish new design of glass-fibre cab was introduced for the Swift GL and Swiftsure HL and PL, also exhibited at the 1958 Show. This had wrap-round windscreen panels and the well-rounded outline was set off by a chromium-plated radiator grille of traditional Thornycroft outline. Sadly, it did little for sales – the lighter models were assembled in a separate workshop with a production-line layout, but in later years it was all too often a very quiet place. Heavier models continued to be built in the main erecting shop, each frame set on trestles and staying there while it was completed by pairs of fitters, whose names appeared on the record for each chassis number.

Gradually, the new glass-fibre cab was adopted for the whole home market range of road-going vehicles. The cab base by then used was almost flat except for the engine cover, and on the larger models the base was slightly wider than the cab top. The Mastiff ML received the new cab by mid-1960, when a six-wheeled Mastiff model, the MH, was also added to the range, designed to run at 20 tons gross. This again had the NS6 or QR6 option, though in this case the latter was almost universal. The chassis had a single driving axle and the type was intended to compete against such models as the AEC Marshal. A production series began with chassis 62596.

Below:
The Mastiff ML received the new-style cab by mid-1960 but remained readily identifiable by its set-back front axle. As with the other larger models, the cab base was also slightly wider than the cab above it. This tipper was an early example. *Thornycroft Society*

Right:
The six-wheeled Mastiff was designated MH, with many chassis features in common with the four-wheeler, though the front axle was not set back. There was a choice of NS6 or QR6 and this example, on chassis number 62604, had the latter. With platform body, it was supplied to Buxton Dawson Ltd in September 1960. *Thornycroft Society*

Below right:
Known within the works simply as 'the dumper', this rugged vehicle was aimed at the construction industry and had a Q6 engine. One is seen here on test on the type of terrain for which it was designed. *Thornycroft Society*

Also announced in mid-1960 was an unnamed model publicised as the heavy-duty 10-13-ton tipper dumper, aimed at the construction industry. It was a stubby high-built half-cab model with 10ft wheelbase, the standard engine being a revised version of the 9.83-litre QR6 engine, designated Q6, also adopted for some of the later Trusty or Mastiff models. Six were built in 1960-1, three going to Scottish Land Development. Another specialised vehicle was a military trench-digger based on the Nubian TFA with B81 engine, built in some numbers in later years.

Left:
The Trusty PK received the new glass-fibre cab from 1960 – this example of the short-wheelbase tipper version on chassis 62348 had the Q6 engine and was delivered in September 1961. *Thornycroft Society*

Below left:
The first of the two prototype Trusty chassis of 1960-1, originally called the PK Mark II, is seen standing in the middle of the erecting shop, ready to move down the works yard to the body shop to receive its cab. This one had the Q6 engine. Various other chassis, including Antar Sandmaster models, can be seen in the early stages of assembly – each chassis was built up on trestles in the charge of a two-man team of fitters. *ATC*

The forward-control Trusty models received the stylish new glass-fibre cab as standard from 1960, but by then work was in hand on what was meant to be a new-generation version of the PK eight-wheeler, at first called the PK Mark II. Initially, it was designed in response to the oil companies' requirement for a 4,000-gallon tanker, which implied a 28-ton gross weight as compared to the limit then in force of 24 tons but on which an indication of a likely future concession had been given by the Ministry of Transport. However, to keep within weight limits for the rear axles, it was necessary for more weight to be transferred to the front axles and these were set back slightly. Various other improvements were incorporated, including the Q6 engine giving 150bhp at 2,200rpm. The prototype was completed by November 1960.

A second, basically similar chassis was also built, but this had a Gardner engine, the first in a post-1945 Thornycroft. This time the engine was of the then recently introduced 6LX type, of 10.45-litre capacity, also giving 150bhp, but at the traditional Gardner 1,700rpm. It seemed that requests from operators who liked the PK chassis but still preferred the Gardner engine were at last being heeded. It was decided that the model designation was now to be T8 instead of PK Mark II. While this vehicle behaved well on test, more fundamental events were occurring. These two chassis had numbers 62678 and 62689, presumed to be in the order described, though the records do not specify engine type or number.

As indicated, the investment made in 1956-8 to get production costs of the Swift and Swiftsure 4-7-ton models down and sales up proved to be based on a forlorn hope, once firms with the resources of Bedford and Ford had begun offering well-developed models with own-make diesel engines in this class. Thornycroft's small output made

Below:
The second of the Trusty prototypes, by then designated T8, with cab and test load, photographed in July 1961. This had a Gardner 6LX engine, the external distinguishing feature at that stage being the external intake to the air cleaner in the side face to the front wing, although later this was repositioned. Over about 7,000 miles of test running, this vehicle was steadily improving in both performance and already outstanding fuel economy, but by then it had been decided not to continue production of home-market Thornycroft models as a consequence of the ACV takeover. *ATC*

Above:
The first of the four prototype 'Ford-Thornycroft' PG/6D
chassis, No 61389, marrying the well-proven Trident PG
13ft 6in-wheelbase frame and running gear to a Ford 6D diesel
engine and Thames Trader controls and cab, seen soon after it
left the erecting shop on 15 June 1960. The other three similar
prototypes, on long-wheelbase, tipper and tractor chassis,
followed later that year. The scheme would have extended
Ford's range to a more substantial class and provided much-
needed volume of work for Thornycroft, as well as possibly
opening the doors to wider co-operation, but it collapsed
mainly due to problems in agreeing on costing methods.
D. B. Pearson

it impossible to avoid high prices, with a resultant further
decline in sales.

What might have been a chance to bridge that gap lay in a
remarkable proposal from Ford, on which design work
began in 1960. That maker's Thames Trader model, itself
covering the 4-7-ton range, with the Ford 6D diesel engine
of 5.4 litres and quite a smartly finished pressed-steel cab,
was proving very successful. However, Ford wanted to
move into a slightly heavier weight range and was interested
in marrying the Thornycroft Trident PG chassis with the
Ford 6D engine, gearbox and cab. The Trident was
considered a well-proven design and its adoption would
enable Ford to save time in designing and developing its
own chassis.

Four prototypes of alternative lengths were built at
Basingstoke, using 6D engines and finished cabs supplied

by Ford, appearing in Thornycroft records as model PG/6D,
with the chassis numbers 61389-92. They were driven to
Ford's test centre and it is understood that they performed
well. Unfortunately, the scheme began falling apart when
Ford's costing staff found that Thornycroft could not
provide the detailed and very precise cost figures which
they expected. Negotiations became bogged down;
meanwhile the ACV takeover described below took effect.
Delivery of the four vehicles is recorded as being in
September 1961, but this may have reflected the final
settlement after the project was terminated. Just what might
have happened had this not been so can only be guessed at –
even if only an interim step for Ford, lasting a few years, it
would surely have provided large-scale work for the
Basingstoke works. Had this have been set up before ACV
arrived on the scene, the eventual outcome might have been
a Ford takeover.

Under New Banners

Sir John E. Thornycroft died on 21 November 1960, and
although he had already relinquished the Chairmanship of
Transport Equipment (Thornycroft) Ltd to Lt-Cdr
J. W. Thornycroft, he remained a powerful figure until the
end. It is significant that the decision to sell this business
came almost immediately after his death – a circular was
sent to shareholders on 15 February 1961 announcing the
sale. The buyer was Associated Commercial Vehicles Ltd,
which was the parent company of the group built around the
AEC concern after Maudslay and Crossley had been taken

over in 1948. The new TE(T) board reflected AEC dominance, though R. F. Newman continued briefly from the previous regime.

For a time, the Thornycroft business at Basingstoke was run as, effectively, a subsidiary of AEC. In some respects, that began to have an impact almost immediately. Direct sales of standard home-market models soon stopped, with a deal under which Oswald Tillotson Ltd, a long-established AEC dealer, took over the sales function for remaining stocks from late 1961. The two T8 prototypes became 'journey vehicles' in the works transport fleet. AEC engine options were being put forward for some export orders by the summer of 1961 – a notable case related to some Trusty VKN tractors for operation in Turkey, where the compact AEC AV690 was chosen, readily fitting into this chassis despite its 11.3-litre capacity, giving the required performance over a hilly route.

In November 1961 it was announced that Thornycroft vehicle output would henceforth be concentrated on specialised models such as the Antar, Big Ben and Nubian – at that stage, the AEC management saw Thornycroft's role as having the same type of relationship as Scammell did to Leyland, the latter then being AEC's main rival. Orders for these types continued to be taken and examples of all were on the company's stand at the 1962 Earl's Court Show.

By then, however, the above logic had been undermined when the whole ACV group was the subject of a further merger, when it became part of the Leyland group in June 1962. Even so, the more direct link to AEC continued to be the principal influence for some time and most of the

Thornycroft machining and unit assembly capability effectively became AEC's main gearbox factory, manufacturing a wide range of manual and epicyclic gearboxes, while the erecting shop continued mainly with the Nubian. Scammell's presence within the group led to a tailing off of Big Ben and Antar orders, and the next generation of tank transporter for the Army was a Scammell. Even so, Antar deliveries continued until 1966, the total Antar output having reached over 730, a remarkable figure for so large a vehicle.

The increasing size of airliners led to a demand for larger and more elaborately equipped crash tenders, and the Nubian Major was introduced in 1964 – 'Major' was reminiscent of AEC practice as a way of indicating a larger but related model. At that date there was no suitable engine in production within the group and the choice went to a Cummins V8, developing up to 300bhp. By 1970, production of the AEC Bush Tractor was set up at Basingstoke, this being a 6x4 model derived from the AEC Dumptruk and designed for use with a semi-trailer to run at 35 tons gross and powered by the AEC AV760 engine of 12.4 litres.

By the early 1970s, British Leyland, as it had become, was running into financial pressures mainly related to the

Below:
The need to cope with potentially larger fires as airliners increased in size led to the development of the Nubian Major, type TMA, a substantially bigger vehicle that the TFA, and powered by a 300bhp Cummins V8 engine. This example was for export to Kenya. *Thornycroft Society*

Austin and Morris car businesses, leading to a policy of retrenchment. In 1972 BL moved out of the Basingstoke works, gearbox production and the bulk of the works being sold to Eaton, the American gearbox specialist – in much the same way, the Maudslay works, by then making axles, passed to Rockwell. The remaining vehicle production, with related specialist staff, moved to the Scammell works at Watford. The British Leyland combine was saved from complete collapse by becoming 99% State-owned in 1974. For a time, the Thornycroft name continued to be used for Watford-built Nubian models, but by 1977 this practice fell victim to a policy of using the Leyland (or sometimes Scammell) name.

Even so, the Nubian survived through the dismantling and selling off of the British Leyland empire, the rights to the Nubian design and the stock of spares being acquired in 1988 by Unipower, also based in Watford.

Meanwhile, in 1966 the former parent company, John I. Thornycroft Ltd, had merged with Vosper Ltd, a boat- and shipbuilding firm with a similarly long history, established in Portsmouth in 1871 though becoming well known for its fast air-sea rescue and motor torpedo boats in World War 2. The new company, Vosper-Thornycroft Ltd, continued its operations at the Woolston shipyard, supplying the Royal Navy with Type 42 destroyers, vastly more complex than their predecessors of earlier times. It became state-owned as part of British Shipbuilders in 1977 but was bought out by its management in 1985. It continues as a leading shipbuilder, notably for the Royal Navy, just as Thornycroft was well over a century ago.

Below:
Production of the AEC Bush Tractor was set up at Basingstoke – 14 of the type are seen in the works yard. For a time, the chassis assembly side of the Basingstoke works operated largely on the lines that it was AEC's specialised vehicle department, producing such vehicles as well as the Nubian Major, the latter continuing to be sold under the Thornycroft name. *Thornycroft Society*

Left:
The end of the line. A Nubian Major chassis was the last vehicle to emerge from the Basingstoke works in 1972. Someone had found the board sometimes carried on No 1 steam van when it was taken out for publicity purposes and rather hastily produced another to mark the occasion. A new chassis-numbering system had been introduced from about 1969, so the continuity of numbering was lost, and in any case by no means all the numbers in the series to 63000-odd were filled, but that sweep of numbers does give some indication of the firm's output in 77 years of vehicle production. *Thornycroft Society*